LETTERS
to HEAVEN

CALVIN MILLER

LETTERS

to HEAVEN

REACHING BEYOND *the* GREAT DIVIDE

WORTHY
PUBLISHING

Published by Worthy Publishing, a division of Worthy Media, Inc., 134 Franklin Road, Suite 200, Brentwood, Tennessee 37027.

HELPING PEOPLE EXPERIENCE THE HEART OF GOD

eBook available at www.worthypublishing.com

Audio distributed through Oasis Audio; visit www.oasisaudio.com

---

Library of Congress Control Number: 2011942286

For foreign and subsidiary rights, contact Riggins International Rights Services, Inc.; www.rigginsrights.com

The author is represented by, and this book is published in association with, the literary agency of WordServe Literary Group, Ltd., www.wordserveliterary.com

ISBN: 978-1-936034-99-4 (trade paper)

Cover Design: Studiogearbox.com
Cover Images: Thinkstock; Veer
Interior Design and Typesetting: Susan Browne Design

Printed in the United States of America
12 13 14 15 16 17 SBI 8 7 6 5 4 3 2

To all those to whom I never got the chance to say good-bye . . .
To any of you to whom I might have given the impression you
were not as significant to me as you really were . . .
To those I prayed for when my prayers were so hurried by my
own to-do agenda, only sympathizing when I should have
empathized . . .
I'm sorry!
I know now I should have laughed with you and meant it.
I should have cried real tears over your own unanswered needs
instead of offering you only shallow pretense.
I should not have dropped off a cheap bowl of fruit and
thought it equal to an honest hour of good conversation.
So . . .
Here's to the psalm we might have shared,
The book we might have read together.
Here's to the evening we missed,
the meeting when I acted like I understood
your brokenness.
Some of you I never met at all, but I would like to
have met you.
We lived on the same planet at vastly different times.
Still, you contributed so much to my life and worldview,
and I wanted you to know that.
But all of you are in heaven now,
And I beg you,
Give me that minute of your time—time I need to finish up
the unfinished business of earth.

—*Calvin Miller*
Still too much at home
on the planet you outgrew

And does my God this place for me prepare?

And will these heavenly pleasures be all mine?

———— ⌘ ————

Thomas Craddock,

1718–1780

CONTENTS

FOREWORD

I saw Eternity the other night,

Like a great ring of pure and endless light.

—— ✺ ——

Henry Vaughn,

1622–1695

How shall I finish up the unfinished business of earth?
Letters, I think.
Each of you who will receive these letters is dead—
    at least in this realm—
    and I am counting on some courier
    whose form of delivery I do not know,
    to get these words through to you.
Most of you I knew well;
    some few of you only a little;
    and some of you I never met at all.
But all of you caused me either solace or pain,
    and I want to be sure that when we meet,
    all of our yesterdays are in a better state of repair
    than they were when you went home.

—C. M.

INTRODUCTION

Heaven is a destiny so grand

that we madly live all our lives

outside its gates

on the porch of hope . . .

waiting to touch the treasure

that is ours inside.

——— ⟨≋⟩ ———

Calvin Miller

Heaven. What's to be done with it? We must have it; otherwise, the end of life is too abrupt to be dealt with and the rest of life too pointless to matter much.

Most every world religion puts some kind of heaven at the end of life. It's a place to get back all we once held and then lost. It's a place to see Grandma again. A chance to make sense of graveyards. It is a place to say with the apostle, "O death, where is your sting?" To Christians, it's a dream of a cup of coffee with the real Jesus we have so long served but never seen.

If I tried to define heaven, I would likely fall into the same trap as people who write serious theological works on the subject. I have read a few of these books, but I almost always get the feeling that the authors are taking their celestial pictures with weak cameras and cheap film, ultimately producing only vague images of God's wondrously vast reality. Apart from the glimpses of heaven that one finds in the Bible, how much more can we know for now? I think Isaiah 55:9 says it best for me, in the Lord's own words: "For as the heavens are higher than the earth, so are My ways higher than your ways, and My thoughts than your thoughts."

So in this book I have not set out to define heaven. Probably when we are actually there, lost in the wonder of the place, we won't much care to define it anyway. Neither is

Letters to Heaven my determination of any person's final destination. That is a matter best left to an all-knowing God and his private work in each individual heart. Instead, this book is about seeing heaven as a place for wrapping up the unfinished business of earth. Beyond the grand gates, everything is resolved. Nothing is ragged at the edge; all the loose threads are tied up.

Clocks and calendars are banned in glory, so no conversation will have deadlines. For as long as we want, we can talk with Jesus. With the patriarchs. With lovers we left in the cemeteries; with friends we haven't seen in years; and yes, with Grandma.

So come with me beyond the Great Divide, where the real glory awaits. Let others chase the metaphors of crystal palaces, pearly gates, and golden streets. The heaven I give you in this book is about people—starting with Jesus, of course. And beyond him, a blessed reunion with mentors, friends, loved ones.

Go ahead and eavesdrop on my conversations with these departed ones; after all, heaven is an eavesdropper's paradise—a completely open, utterly healing land with no secrets. Walk with me where none of us have ever been, and let's pray for each other—that we may live and love well now, on our way to finishing up the unfinished business of earth.

MEETING MAMA'S GOD

Mama loved . . . the God on whom a desperate

mother might call when she was out of

ideas on how to hold her world together.

—— ⟋⟍⟋ ——

C. M.,

Life Is Mostly Edges

ETHEL
MILLER

Who can tell all the reasons mothers love their sons? Maybe it was because I was the little boy bewildered by your divorce in 1941. Or perhaps because a child gives his mother an important reason to *be* when the world caves in and she finds herself all alone facing an uncertain future.

There is no question; I have always been a mama's boy. It was hard not to magnify your role in the survival of our family of nine, especially during the World War II years. By the end of those years, I was a convert to Christianity as a nine-year-old boy. And then came junior high and high school, college and then graduate school, and then the Christian ministry as a pastor of a very large church. Somewhere in this mini-history of my life, I found your undeserved esteem for me one of the most rewarding assets of my being.

But I was never much at ease with the way I felt your pride in my education and career. It might have been that I was the first of your children to earn a college degree. It might have been the fact that I became the pastor of a relatively large church. But at each successive milestone and each new step of my career, I found you quietly proud of me as though I had arrived at each of those plateaus on my own, a self-made man.

The truth is, I am not. I never told you—at least not often enough to make you believe it—that there were only two forces behind any excellence I ever attained. The first was Jesus! I am not just saying this to sound humble or religious. From the time I was little, my own insecurity in the world caused me to want to trust in God. I was not a brave teenager. I was not a forthright athlete, confident I could achieve anything. Somehow I felt that unless I could become a partner with God, I would never make it. I lacked the strength to believe in myself, and as a result I increasingly turned to God for strength and confidence. With Christ, I managed to keep my eye on the ball; my desire to please him with my life, I am sure, pushed me into any arena of esteem I ever received.

The second force, Mama, was you. I have a feeling that mothers get so used to serving their families in their workaday worlds that they never see the power of their influence. The best teaching isn't done in formal classes that begin and end with the flow of terms and semesters. There are no credit courses that start with diapers and culminate in high-school diplomas. It's the steadiness of motherhood that makes the point: the lullabies that mothers rarely see as music or the endless washing of little faces that the best of mothers never call hygiene. The Q-and-A proceeding from "Why?" and "But why?" that mothers never call Education 101. The correction for bad language that mothers rarely call ethics. All these things are the most important part of our education.

Mama, when you read *A Christmas Carol* to us, you never called it English Lit. It was just together time. When you read the paper, it was never Current Events. When you explained why you were a Democrat, we never called it American Government. When you went to vote, you never called it Civics. But bit by bit we were putting together a worldview, all under the most careful eye of a great moralist and Christian—only it never came across that way.

Now I can see that my life for these past seventy-some years was the product of that special relationship I found in Jesus and yourself. And what I liked best about it was that you never resented Jesus for the special place he held as Master of my life.

I will never forget the time I came home from that pentecostal revival and announced, "I've been saved!" My exuberance must have amused you, and yet you saw the moment as the most important of my life. I was never casual about Jesus. I wanted to know what he thought about me, about my moral choices, about the ultimate direction of my life.

The same went for you, Mama. I cared about what you thought about where I wanted to go, what I wanted to be. When I told you I was going to a Baptist college in Oklahoma, you seemed excited about the dream. It was one of the most expensive private schools in the state, yet you seemed pleased that I had the dream, and you knew that it emanated from the Christ who occupied the center of my intention.

Well, you've been in heaven with Christ for thirty-three years now, and I can see that I am on my way there too. But I wanted to send this letter on ahead to set up our coming reunion. I want to begin heaven a little more realistically than I lived things out down here. I don't see how Jesus will have the kind of time I want to spend with the both of you. Still, if you can arrange for the three of us to meet, it would make a great beginning of our time together.

I wrote a good bit of poetry on your mentoring life, but alas, only after you were gone. One poem comes to mind even now.

To Mama and Jesus,
You and He,

You gave me life and He extended it.

You saved me from the cold and He from sin.

You taught me hope and He defended it.

From you I once was born . . . from Him again.

You let me skip in fields that He had made.

He bid me bless the loaves you baked for me.

You ordered me to gaze where once He lay.

He bid me kneel in your Gethsemane.

I owe you both the treasure of my art.

I myself am so saddled with this debt

That I cannot fail in paying every part

Lest I should leave this pair with one regret.

You, Mother, taught me how to love a King.

In both of you was hidden everything.

Mama, you live in a higher realm of poetry than I could ever write. But if you will, please show that poem to Jesus. I think he'd be as interested in it as you. You both seemed to love me so.

TO A MAN WHOSE GOD
WAS ON THE GRIDIRON

The gods assemble on the gridiron

To sanctify Sunday for men grown weary of church.

—— ⟨∾∾∾⟩ ——

James Kavanaugh,

"The Football Game"

ou went to heaven from a ringside seat, close up, at the
fifty-yard line.

At least I hope you went to heaven. The only reason I
have my doubts is that you never had much of an appe-
tite for heaven. And frankly, Ed, I have long wondered if
anyone who has not the slightest desire to go to heaven
can ever end up there. But I am hoping you get this letter
because I know if you do, then (by this time) you will have
changed your mind about the place.

I will never forget the day you died. Your family wanted
me to visit you in the hospital and talk to you about making
a last confession and, as we evangelicals are wont to say, to
accept Christ as your Savior. It was a great attempt, the last
hurrah, the hope of your family that in your final moments
of life you might declare yourself for God and make some

kind of confession that you were embracing the faith. It was not my only time to seek this confession from you. I had done so many times, always at your family's prodding, but all to no avail.

In every seminar I ever attended on how to lead someone to Christ—and in every one I ever taught—I was always told to get to know the prospective Christian and then press upon him or her the good confession. But I had talked with you so often that I felt I already had really gotten to know you. I knew you had one great love in life, and it wasn't God. It was Nebraska football! You knew the names and numbers of all the players as well as I knew the name of all the apostles.

Obviously, we came at life from two different priority points. Coach Tom Osborne was your infallible guide to meaning. I picked Jesus of Nazareth.

From the very first, we each considered the other a dull conversationalist. You probably didn't answer the door when I stopped by because you saw me as a pushy Baptist who was gonna "talk Jesus" at you. Meanwhile, I didn't really want to come by because I thought you were the most off-the-track, football-fanatical cancer victim that ever existed. You couldn't understand why anyone could actually love God so much if he forbade them any real interest in sports. You were much more fluent in profanity than I was, and I think you heaped up your argument with four-letter words that you knew would nettle me—perhaps to the extent I would quit coming by. And I would have, except that your family was so anxious for you to become a Christian before you died, no matter that you had no real interest in Jesus.

During your final week of life, they asked me to make one more attempt. I understood that their greatest desire was a goal of your least interest. Yet as I had before, I geared myself up and went to the hospital where you would remain until your death.

As usual, you greeted me with contempt.

I would have preferred you saying hello when we met, rather than "Oh #*~#, not you again!"

"Hello, my good friend, how are you?"

"Now why would you say that, #*~#? I'm not your good friend. I don't even like you."

"The doc says you're not doing well," I said. "Thought we might have a little talk."

"I know what you want to talk about! My kids think I'm on the way to hell! And I probably am, but I'd sure like a little peace and quiet along the way. I know I could never talk you out of it, seeing you are determined to carve another notch in your Bible. So I'm gonna shut up and listen. I haven't got the strength to do anything more, but I'd like to walk out of here and just avoid the conversation."

"Is it okay, then, if I walk you through some pretty important verses? Your family wants me to do this."

"I'll shut up, and you talk," was all you said.

I can't tell you how much I struggled to find the desire to talk to you. I've seen a lot of men on the brink of hell, but none as seemingly pleased with being in that position as you. In some ways, Ed, you knew you were going to hell, and you knew what hell was all about. Still, you were defiant to the end.

What I knew that you didn't guess was the strength of the love of God. But I couldn't make that real to you.

God is indeed love, and he is so committed to saving the human race that he hangs between heaven and hell and throws up a million roadblocks to keep anyone from dying outside of his all-compelling love. Still, he is so big on individual liberty that he forces no one's hand. God is not willing "that any should perish but that all should come to repentance" (2 Peter 3:9). But the unrepentant still hold the upper hand. More than that, God hangs about the precipice of death and weeps when men and women of self walk over it.

Years ago, in *The Singer*, I imagined a conversation in which an obstinate person, perhaps as obstinate as Ed, asked God to mercifully decide the matter—send him off to hell and lock him up forever.

In that imagined conversation, God refused the sinner's request. "I have never desired to send anyone to hell," said God, "but if you insist on going there, I would never lock you out."[1]

Perhaps because you were losing your vitality, you grew quiet. I said all that is most important to hear when one is balanced on the edge of life. You listened. In fact, it seemed you *really* listened, maybe for the first time, maybe thanks to the lateness of the hour and that awful corridor of weakened blood pressure that was threatening you with common sense. You were in that valley of the shadow where the oscilloscope is zigzagging its way across your electrocardiogram. I hate that horrible flat-line moment that stops the zigzag as the oxygen ceases its wheezing inside the plastic mask.

When I had finished telling the old, old story, I somehow felt for a moment that I was about to witness the miracle for which your whole family had been praying. You were too weak to talk, but it appeared that you were lifting your hand. It was a palsied and very shaky movement, but you were actually using your last bit of strength to raise your hand. It looked as if you were smiling through the plastic oxygen mask. I could all but hear the angels singing.

Then you laid your unsure hand on the TV control unit. I was sure you were going to say, "I believe!"

Instead what you said was, "Big Red!"—the colloquial name of the Cornhusker football team.

I was so stupid as to forget that it was two o'clock on Saturday—kickoff time at the stadium in Lincoln. You were only raising your hand to turn on the football game.

I mumbled a final prayer for you, but it was too quiet to be heard above the roar of the television.

"Big Red!" were the last words I ever heard you say in this world. But then I have always believed that deathbed conversion attempts have too much going against them to ever be consistently effective. People die pretty much as they have lived.

Ironically, Tom Osborne, the Nebraska coach, was well-known for being a Christian. I've always wondered what would have happened if he could have made that last call on you. If he, the centerpiece of your adulation, had told you how much Christ meant to him—and I know that was a great deal—you might have borrowed from his faith just enough to help you through the gates. But he was busy, over at the stadium in Lincoln. And you were too attached to your oxygen to be anywhere else except in a hospital bed.

Still, I have labored all these years, hoping that maybe, after the game—in your final moments of consciousness— you set the angels singing, and your weeping Father in heaven caught you by the shoulders as you passed the

gates, and said to you, "Well done, good and faithful ser-
vant; you have been faithful over a few things, I will make
you ruler over many" (Matthew 25:21).

I cling to the hope that, somewhere in the last seconds
of the game, you called Christ "Lord" and that this letter,
addressed to Ed Pattison in heaven, has found you at the
only worthy address eternity has to offer.

THE ROAR OF IMPACT, THE HUSH OF HEAVEN

I know that Todd is in heaven, and I know

that I'm going to see him again and that his

efforts were not in vain. Evil in this world

will ultimately be conquered by God.

———— ∞ ————

Lisa Beamer,
Let's Roll

TODD
BEAMER

I can easily imagine your entering into heaven on September 11, 2001. I can even imagine how quickly you adjusted to your new home. But I struggle to imagine that fiery finale in an open field near Shanksville, Pennsylvania, where Flight 93 plowed into the earth in a curtain of flame, erupting from the fifty-foot-deep trench your plane plowed into the earth.

Here is a big thank you from me—and the only place I can deliver it is to send it to your new mansion in heaven. How much we Americans owe you and your fellow flyers, Todd.

I was recently in Washington, D.C., and as I gazed at the Capitol and the White House, I didn't think of the presidents or the noble men and women of Congress. I thought of you. I thought of that incident that made you and your comrades the icons of courage you proved to be. It was your moment, but it was a huge moment for all of us.

As the towers fell on 9/11, you and those other heroes on Flight 93 thwarted the hijackers' plans to fly yet another plane into yet another building. And not just any building, but our Capitol or the White House. You forced your way into the cockpit and forced the plane to earth near Shanksville. I have read of that moment when you charged toward the cockpit. The story was given to the world by Airfone switchboard operator Lisa Jefferson, who told your wife— your own Lisa—about the call you made that day when you couldn't reach your wife. The story describes how you spent your courage to save our country.

I can hardly wait to thank you personally for the stewardship of your daring.

I love your tentative willingness to do something, and your pausing to ask yourself if you were up to it. "We're going to do something," you told Lisa Jefferson, and not much later you added, "It's what we have to do!"

Lisa Jefferson said you asked her to pray the Lord's Prayer with you. And when the time for praying was over, it was time to play the man—a man for all time, and a man for all of history. A simple man, a handsome, winsome Christian! Unsure of yourself, yet, it would seem, a man of utter confidence in God, for Lisa Jefferson heard you say over the phone, "Jesus, help me!"

And so he did. He helped you to preserve the republic.

Todd, heaven is the place where you are going to meet a lot of admirers you never knew you had. Americans agree: you and the other heroes of Shanksville were brilliant patriots and martyrs. You played the role of ordinary men who saved a nation.

But, Todd, it was Lisa Jefferson who said the assault on the hijackers began when you cried out, "Let's roll!" And it was your own dear wife who said, "The courageous action of the passengers and the crew reminded me on that day when people around the world felt violated, helpless, alone and afraid, there were still people of character, people who in the midst of crisis dared to live to the last second with hope."[1]

I met your wife at a booksellers' convention in 2002. Like almost everyone who attended that event, I had a huge desire to shake her hand. I am not your customary groupie, but like all good Americans, the Beamers had come to stand for something so courageous and so all-American, I couldn't help myself.

We talked less than five minutes, but it was long enough for me to sense that the woman behind the man was in and of herself heroic. She is a beautiful woman, Todd, and more than just physically so. She is the kind of person who makes you feel glad she is on the planet, her commitment to Christ and family canceling out the unwholesome elements of those whose commitment is not so exemplary.

I looked over the pictures of you and her and the children, and I realized that a Christian marriage is a gift to a world that needs to see what the best of human commitment looks like. I guess the most touching thing about Lisa's book celebrating your courage was the account of her trip to the Shanksville crash site. Her words made me think of those little crosses erected by the roadside where a loved one died in an automobile accident. For twenty years my family had a second home in New Mexico, and I suppose there isn't a highway in the state I haven't been down. Wherever I roamed, I always would see those little white crosses, made bright and almost gaudy with plastic floral arrangements, along the highway. I've heard people say they never liked those little crosses. But I knew why the families placed them there. It is the same reason we go to the cemetery on Memorial Day. It's not that we believe our loved ones are there; it is somehow a place of remembering them. I never believed in making such visits very much till my own beloved mother went to heaven. Now not a year goes by that I don't visit her headstone.

Lisa's September 17, 2001, account of visiting the Shanksville site was gripping to read. She wrote that as she prepared to leave the site of the memorial service there, she eyed a hawk soaring above the field where the plane had crashed. The sight filled her with an overwhelming peace that brought the words of Isaiah 40:30–31 to her mind:[2]

> Even the youths shall faint and be weary,
> And the young men shall utterly fall,
> But those who wait on the LORD
> Shall renew their strength;
> They shall mount up with wings like eagles,
> They shall run and not be weary,
> They shall walk and not faint.

"Never before in my life had the difference between those who put their hope in God and those who put their hope in this world been so obvious to me," Lisa wrote. "My family and I mourned the loss of Todd deeply that day . . . and we still do. But because we hope in the Lord, we know beyond a doubt that we will see Todd again."[3]

Todd, I don't know if your daily rounds in the glorious eternity you have inherited leaves you missing your earthly friends and your wonderful family. But the heart-adoration we give to Jesus puts that desire front and center in our lives. Of course, we want to see our Savior in that land where there are no more tears, no more terrorists, and no more plane crashes. But we also want to see those who have preceded us in hope. I know a wonderful reunion is on the way for the Beamers. And confidentially, if I could have my way, I would like to see you someday in that bright land too.

The joy I felt as I shook Lisa's hand that day in 2002, I want to experience again in shaking your hand. The hero you never meant to be became a legend in the world you had to leave. I suspect it will be a busy day for you to shake the hand of all those who admire you. But look carefully: I'll be one of those in line.

TO THE WOMAN
WHO TAUGHT ME
ILLEGALLY

God has not created me for naught.

—— ⌘ ——

John Henry Newman,

1801–1890

ROWENA STRICKLAND

D ear elder sister, you and I have unfinished business. When I enrolled in your freshman Bible survey, I was immediately enthralled with your ability to take my ignorance about Scripture and show me that I was naïve to the point of immaturity. We were both evangelicals and, to be frank, at that time in my life I thought that to be evangelical was to be like Jesus, who himself was—I believed—an evangelical.

I was seventeen when you dropped a bomb on my untried theology. You blurted the obscene truth right out loud: Jesus was a *Hebrew*. I was utterly amazed to discover that Jesus was a Jew and to hear you discuss his authenticity on the basis of his Jewishness. You blew my mind.

Thank you. It needed blowing. In fact, my mind theretofore had pursued only the narrowest truth within some very high Baptist walls.

I am sure it had come up somewhere in an adolescent Sunday school class that Jesus was a Jew, but I had somehow missed it. Dr. Strickland, I know you must have sensed my naiveté. I can't have been the first rural Oklahoma greenhorn you ever saw. And you were dedicated to breaking the truth to me gently. I had always thought of Jesus as a Baptist who therefore didn't dance, go to movies, or play canasta. He, of course, went to Baptist revivals and potluck dinners at the church.

Not a Jew! It couldn't possibly be!

It was a hard pill to swallow, but I managed the medicine I needed to get clear of my ignorance. Still, I had barely come to accept the Jewishness of Jesus when you dropped a second bomb. You said that we were all part of the Judeo-Christian tradition. I'm sorry, but that was just too much! And then you said . . . Jesus never went to Sunday school!

I had to go back to the dormitory and lie down. These are the kinds of things you don't get over all at once.

But there was even more to come: you also taught me that he was a field rabbi. You might as well have said he was a Methodist.

For a while, I eyed you with suspicion. You were clearly

a liberal. But then I should have suspected that. After all, you were a *woman* teaching the Bible. My pastor had warned me about women Bible teachers. There was quite a movement going on against them. Baptists never really burned any women at the stake, but the notion was afoot that women who taught Scripture should explore Methodism, which had its own liberal college in Winfield and was clearly the denomination in which women could find acceptance. At least that was how my pastor felt about women professors. He quoted me a really important verse of Scripture from the King James Bible:

> Let a woman learn in silence with all subjection. But I suffer not a woman to teach, nor to usurp authority over the man, but to be in silence. . . . Notwithstanding she shall be saved in childbearing, if they continue in faith and charity and holiness with sobriety. (1 Timothy 2:11–12,15)

Suddenly I could see it, Dr. Strickland. As we might have said in my Oklahoma family back then, you done usurped authority over me! I wasn't even sure you could be saved since you had never had a child and, according to the text, you could only be saved in childbearing. Your heresy deserved a challenge—you were a childless authority usurper!

I wasn't the only one suspicious of your heresies. There were other skeptics in the crowd as well. Other seventeen-year-old scholars from important wheat-belt theological centers like Tecumseh and Blackwell and Osawatomie.

I think September 1954 was the hardest month of my life. I wanted to be true to the Word, and I think I even wanted to be nice to you, but you were laying a lot of stuff on my flimsy worldview. I had to adjust to the fact that I was not just a Baptist any longer; I was a Judeo-Christian, and I had to try to figure out how Jesus could be a somewhat decent Savior when he never went to Sunday school.

In those days I believed God had called me to be a Baptist missionary, but what kind of missionary would I be? A Judeo-Christian missionary? How would I ever convert the heathen? What is the Swahili word for Judeo-Christian?

I might have left college and remained forever in ignorance had it not been for your kindness. That was the one thing that kept me studying with you. You were a heretic—anyone could see that. But you were so darn nice! Further, you really seemed to like me. You took time for me after class, and we talked about Jesus and how nice he was (even if he was a Jew!). And you were nice too. Sometimes I would leave one of your lectures thinking, *Well, she may be a liberal, but I don't have too many friends, and a liberal professor who likes me is probably more to be esteemed than an orthodox teacher who doesn't.*

Ultimately, I came to a theological showdown with my pastor. "How are your Bible classes going at the college?" he asked me.

"Good!" I said. "By the way, did you know Jesus was a Jew?"

"Yeah! I knew it!" he said.

"Well, how come you never told me? I've been going to this church for six years, and you never once told me. In fact, you always told me the Jews put Jesus to death. That might have been a good place to bring up the fact that Jesus himself was a Jew!"

"Has that Dr. Strickland messed up your mind?"

"Not much. You know I've always been a Baptist, but I'm getting real close to being a Judeo-Christian!"

"I thought it would come to this! I just want to remind you that our church is paying a part of your tuition, and we might have to reconsider continuing your support if you leave the Baptist church."

I assured him I could be a Judeo-Christian and a Baptist at the same time. In fact, Rowena, that's what you were. Secretly, I thought that, except for the issue of gender, I wanted to be like you.

In time, the pastor got down off his high horse and decided that even if women shouldn't be Bible teachers, they at least had a right to live. Further, the church never did cancel my scholarship, and I finished four years later with flying colors and great grades, even in my Bible survey courses. Twenty years later my children went to that same college. They knew that Jesus was a Jew because I had told them when they were little, but just in case they got real mixed up, I told them to enroll in your Bible survey classes, which they did. And I told them not to be afraid of being Judeo-Christians. It isn't as bad as it sounds.

Since then we've all moved on with our lives, and you have moved on to heaven, Rowena. I know heaven's glad of it.

You probably know this, but my daughter Melanie married a preacher, and Tim is a missionary in Peru. For Baptist kids, they have made terrific Judeo-Christians.

CANCER VICTOR

I was thinking I would miss the rain. I wonder

if you can experience the rain in heaven, if God

will let you dip your wings down. . . . But my

biggest expectation now is just to live. I will not

go gently into that good night.

—— ✎ ——

Farrah Fawcett,
Farrah's Story

FARRAH
FAWCETT

I have only met a handful of famous people in my life, and of movie stars, only a few. Perhaps that is why Thanksgiving dinner in 1969 was a holiday I will long remember. Your sister was a member of our very small church in Omaha, and my children, who were six and seven years old at the time, were a part of the festivities that Thanksgiving Day. Your career was as young as you, and while your name had been bandied about a bit, you were not as well known as you were destined to become.

Your sister insisted that we join your family for dinner. We only lived a few blocks away, and since our church was so small at that time, we were grateful for the invitation. The children were too young to know much about the motion picture industry, but they understood perfectly when we told them you were a movie star. Both of them wanted to sit by you at dinner, and we saw your warm glimmer of approval at their forwardness. It was probably true that you were so new at being a star that you realized it would be a real kick for them—as it may have turned out to be for you as well.

Thanksgiving! Glorious it was! We read the "Old 100th" psalm and had prayer and began to eat. I was struck by how stunningly beautiful you were. But it was more than just physical beauty. There was a hint of grace and self-condescension about you. You seemed to enjoy the meal and the conversation—even the children—as if we were the stars and you were the one impressed with us.

We talked about your role in Blake Edwards's forthcoming *Myra Breckinridge*, the movie version of Gore Vidal's novel that was about to break upon the world in 1970. Your sister made us all promise that we would see the film as close to opening day as possible. We all "crossed our hearts and hoped to die" if we did not fulfill the pledge to catch the film at its debut in Omaha.

It was genuinely a great day for remembering the blessings from God that had carried you to national prominence and had afforded us all the privilege of the day and the honor of celebrating God's good gifts together. There was so much to talk about that the sunset seemed to come early that crisp day, and soon the glow of the lights reflected the warmth of the day. After much delay and a second round of pumpkin pie and coffee, it was time for us to go. Even as we left the house, your sister made us promise once again that we would see your movie when it came out.

The day was gone, but not my memory of it. Here's the part of the story that you never knew, Farrah.

When your movie released, for reasons I can't recall, I couldn't make it to opening night. But it was a smash hit.

Myra Breckenridge was nominated for six Golden Globe awards; it won four. The movie was a boon to your career. But the best thing that happened that Thanksgiving season, in my opinion, was that you, Farrah, became a favorite of the Millers.

Still, I must confess, dear famous sister of us all, it was the classy way you left us that most impressed and thrilled me—with your legacy and with the gift you gave us. Your struggle with cancer seemed to all of us to be a pilgrimage into the unknown shared with the whole world. You left us a torch for the journey that sooner or later belongs to us all.

But as so often happens, the clarity of life's lessons is blunted by the news of the day. Both you and Michael Jackson died on June 25, 2009. The pop singer's international acclaim eclipsed the lessons your own passing might have achieved had things been otherwise. In a 1980 interview, just as your career was really being born, Barbara Walters asked how you would rate your own beauty on a scale of one to ten.

"A nine. . . . Barely a nine. I was going to say eight-and-a-half, but I think fractions aren't all that good," you told Walters. "I think you have to have all of me in order to think that I'm beautiful. In other words, it's not just my looks. I think I have to speak and move and relate for you to feel that . . . for you to feel beauty from me."

I realize that your passing generated little attention from America's evangelicals. There are, after all, heroes in every avenue of life, and mine are always those who gave Christ all. But I remember you years before the priest gave you your last rites, and I agree with your own assessment: Beauty is more than skin deep; it is soul deep. And we all need to relate to someone else to widen our definition of true beauty.

That's what I learned from you forty-one years before you left us. That's what I came to see on the Thanksgiving we shared back in 1969.

Thank you for a larger definition of beauty. Your definition is truly one washed in grace.

THE MAN WHO CELEBRATED CORPUSCLES

What is the use of preserving my old body if it

is not going to be used where God needs me?

———— ❦ ————

The wisdom of Granny Brand,

quoted in *In His Image*

P aul, though I served a couple of times on conference programs with you—eating breakfast, lunch, and dinner with you for the better part of a week—I never felt completely at ease calling you Paul. My admiration for you made me feel that you deserved more respect than any use of your first name. After all, I had read all those marvelous books you wrote with Phil Yancey, and their virile and creative style left me in awe of you both.

It was at one particular conference—just outside of Bellingham, Washington, I think—that you gave me two priceless gifts. I believe I thanked you for them, but if I did not make my gratitude clear, I would like to thank you again. You have been in heaven for a decade now, and if I neglected to say thanks back then, I would like to say it now.

The first gift you gave me was the camaraderie we

found in reflecting on the greatest spiritual and moral influence of both our lives: our mothers.

At the time of our common sojourn, I had recently lost my own mother. She had, some short years earlier, gone to be with the Lord, and her passing was much on my mind all through the week you and I were together at the conference. So it was only natural that I should frequently recall my reminiscences about my mother, as you did yours. We were both older men even then, but clearly our conversations flew to the memories of those women who our lives celebrated. I learned that week that even old men remain, in the best sense of the word, mama's boys.

In your book *In His Image*, I had read of your esteem for your mother:

> In old age my mother had little physical beauty left in her. . . . The rugged conditions in India, combined with crippling falls and her battles with typhoid, dysentery, and malaria, had made her a thin, hunched-over old woman . . . with wrinkles as deep and extensive as any I have seen on a human face.[1]

A few years before you wrote your terrific tribute to your mother, I had written my tribute of my own mother in *A Covenant for All Seasons*:

In her confident presence, I grew up braver than I might have been. I never knew I was poor, either. . . . From time to time there are those who do spin straw into gold. She was one of those who could create a sense of strong abundance from the thinnest poverty. . . . She gave dignity to thrift. She taught all her children to feel pride in constructing the indispensible from the things that others threw away. . . . Hand-me-downs from my two older brothers were an opportunity to wear things that had already twice proven themselves worthy.[2]

As we lingered after breakfast and rehearsed the nobility of motherhood in general and our own mothers in particular, I was struck by the similarity of our esteem for these iconic women, both humble and yet forceful in our development.

I don't remember that we talked about this, but it was about that time when I began to see how Oriental cultures first arrived at ancestor worship. It is hard to avoid reshaping the idolatry of motherhood into one's own household Baal. Of course, we didn't go overboard with our exaltation, but we did freely admit that it was they who had helped to form a sense of virtue in both our lives. Not in what we were, exactly, but certainly in what we wanted to be.

You and your beloved Granny Brand were reunited in heaven in 2003, and my own reunion with my mother is still pending. And other than seeing Christ himself, one should want to see again the wonderful earthly women who could fashion heaven in the middle of our souls.

But there is one other gift for which I must thank you: the gift of esteem you had for the human body. No other religion in the world seems to so exalt the human body as much as Christianity does. Psalm 139:14 seemed to be for you a creed for all health-science professionals. Christ's own body, so often lambasted by gnostics as too much of the Spirit and too little of the earth, led them to develop a "ghostly" Christ, never fully flesh enough to be a real man. But John the Evangelist warred against this anemic, surreal Christ by showing him doing things all human beings do.

Christianity has always been a force for honoring the human body. At the end of the first Christian century, the gnostic heretics did their most to downplay the importance of our physical bodies in favor of our more spiritual selves. Jesus rose bodily from the dead. It wasn't just his spirit, aqueous and filmy, that walked out of the tomb. His body did. His body was missing from the tomb. Everyone could see that! That Jesus had a body is the whole point of the doctrine of the empty tomb.

He was a man, and fully so. Jesus ate and slept and in general was fully human. John actually said so in the beginning of his Gospel when he wrote, "The Word became flesh and dwelt among us" (John 1:14). Jesus was real flesh and blood, a true human being. Very God, but very man as well. As a man, Jesus got thirsty (John 19:28), had his side lanced (John 19:34), ate a piece of fish (Luke 24:42), and cooked breakfast by the sea (John 21:12).

And not only was his body solid enough to cook breakfast by the Sea of Galilee, but it was so real he could invite Thomas to put his finger into the nail-prints of his very human hands. Ghosts can do none of those things.

Adam and Eve's creation was surely, for you, the most intricate and glorious event of Eden. But suddenly, while listening to your lectures and then talking endlessly about their content, I felt a dynamic new idea. Well, it wasn't really a new idea. It was an idea as old as the New Testament itself.

Paul was the first to give us doctrines as to the importance of the body: Colossians 2:9 says that on Christ descended "all the fullness of the Godhead *bodily*" (emphasis is mine). Further, Paul's picture of the Second Coming has dead Christians rising first from their graves.

Paul does his best to say that after death our next body will be transformed and more "spiritual" but a body nonetheless:

> There are . . . heavenly bodies and there are earthly
> bodies; but the splendor of the heavenly bodies is

one kind, and the splendor of the earthly bodies is another. . . . So it will be with the resurrection of the dead. The body that is sown is perishable, it is raised imperishable; it is sown in dishonor, it is raised in glory; it is sown in weakness, it is raised in power; it is sown a natural body, it is raised a spiritual body. . . . Listen, I tell you a mystery: We will not all sleep, but we will all be changed. . . . For the perishable must clothe itself with the imperishable, and the mortal with immortality. (1 Corinthians 15:40, 42–44, 51, 53 NIV)

Yet in all of this there is a reverence for the body. Just as the body of the post-resurrected Christ was different than the one he had before, so all of those who die in Christ will enjoy a new kind of life, but somehow the body remains.

Paul, it was your gift to me to see that whether or not we're in heaven or on earth, the whole idea of bodies is wonderful. In our merely created state—cells, protoplasm, and the like—we are truly "fearfully and wonderfully made" (Psalm 139:14). There is sheer miracle in the form and force of the human body. You had a way of exalting particular aspects of our bodies, showing that our physiology was nothing short of miraculous. You would often open your sermons by saying something strikingly uncanny about how we were so incredibly created, and pointing to the simple things about our bodies that were truly glorious.

One of the nights during the wonderful week of that conference, you opened your sermon by asking, "How many of you have thanked God today for your corpuscles?"

It was an overwhelming statement. It had been years since I had even thought of my corpuscles. Most of us in the audience looked down ashamed, because we knew what was coming next: "Shame on you," you said with a wry smile. "Think of all they accomplish that is responsible for why you are here, so alert and so alive. And it's all because of your corpuscles."

There followed a whole litany of wonder dedicated to the corpuscles. As I recall, you said something like this: "These little red cells start out in a great gush of red and leap from your ventricle into the eight-lane highway of the aorta. And then they swim like crazy to the four-lane brachial artery; then they take a two-lane road down to the exit ramp where they find first a little lane and then a narrow footpath of a vessel before they come to a culvert of a capillary. There they fold themselves double and crawl into the capillary, dump the oxygen, sweep up the trash, and then hurry off to the liver, the spleen, the kidneys, and the lungs. Then, when they are once again bright red with oxygen, they jump back into the ventricle and are off again."

In your book you reminded us that "sixty thousand

miles of blood vessels link every living cell." Our red blood cells rush through this network "until finally the red cell must bow sideways and edge through a capillary one-tenth the diameter of a human hair. . . . The pell-mell journey, even to the extremity of the big toe, lasts a mere twenty seconds." The journey ends in the spleen, you said, where "the battered cell is stripped bare by scavenger cells and recycled into new cells. Three hundred billion such cells die and are replaced every day."[3]

I must confess, I was stunned.

Until I heard your sermon, I had never realized how much I took my physiology for granted. But I determined I wouldn't do that anymore. And then the real miracle occurred. I couldn't think about anything but corpuscles the rest of that evening. I write a lot of children's poems, and as I lay awake that night pondering your exposé of corpuscles, I suddenly got up and wrote a children's poem about them. It wasn't brilliant, but it did support my theory that the muses' best dancing sometimes occurs in the middle of the night.

I finished the poem in almost no time, and then I read it to you the next morning at breakfast, and when you asked me if you could keep it, I was more than honored. I can't be sure how much it meant to you, but I think a great deal. I always wondered if you used it in that wonderful sermon from then on. I do know that from that moment on, we were pen pals, at first frequently and then, ever after, less regularly. We exchanged notes at least once every Christmas until you went to heaven. And when I read of your death, I couldn't help but think, *Isn't heaven lucky?*

I'm only guessing you don't need corpuscles too much in heaven, but they are busy keeping the world functioning down here. Sometimes, at a public reading, I share the little poem and tell the story of the night you made me aware of the human body, and what a great compliment it was when the Word became flesh and God thought of such a wonderful way to keep it alive.

I'm sorry for our sakes that you are no longer on the planet, but I'm keeping your wonderful lecture alive as best I can. And it is glorious work to speak for you in your absence.

There are things too little to see if you please,
That wiggle and wriggle inside arteries.
They vibrate and spin and go buzz in your blood,
And all through your body they hurry and scurry.
Be thankful they're there—they all have red hair—
And by millions and jillions they make your blood red.
Believe me, if they ever took the day off,
In seventeen seconds you'd be very dead.
So tonight when you say your nighty-night prayers,

Say, "God, I'm most grateful for these little spuds,
These little red doo-dads that buzz in my blood.
And, God, if you keep those guys swimming all night.
I'll get up and thank you as soon as it's light."

We are truly fearfully and wonderfully made.

A LESSON ON
HUGGING GENERALS

*Ruby Bridges . . . faced the barricades when
the forced integration of the school system was
occurring. . . . It was a miracle to see this beautiful
little African-American girl pass through the
leering ugly faces of white defiance and continue
on into the school. . . . When others asked Ruby
how she had managed to pass the barricades,
with a smiling confidence she simply said she
prayed. . . . It is perhaps believing children who
best teach us the practice of the presence of God.*

— ◦∾◦ —

Calvin Miller,
Jesus Loves Me

MIFFY
THOMAS

Miffy, it has been a long time now since you went to heaven, but I've never forgotten that bleak Nebraska day when you left us. We were such good friends that you always stood by me when I greeted the church members on their way out of services. You lit up our small church with your perpetual discipline of joy. So unpracticed. So real. Happiness was the aura you wore upon your jumpers and winter corduroys. You had time for everyone. You were never in a hurry—at least until it was time for you to show up in heaven. Then you left us all at once. No time for one of your flamboyant and showy hugs. You simply left before any of us could kiss you good-bye.

I was shocked when your papa called me to tell me you were gone. The news was hard to gather up and even harder to believe. God is never easy to understand, but this was so very baffling. I could understand why God called you home—your innate innocence and joy would brighten up the place. But what did he have against the rest of us? Earth can be a little dingy and ill-lit at times.

Loving Jesus when we die is the rule. A long, long earthly life is somehow the best front porch of foreverness. But children are not meant to die young. Heaven is quite often a matter of theological speculation for those who have never lost a child. But it is never so academic to those who have.

It was for this reason that I found myself in a quandary as I prepared to officiate at your funeral. You challenged my credulity—really, my ability. I have preached children's funerals before, and they are never easy. It always makes me wonder why someone with my lifetime of perverse confessions has the right to look childish innocence in the heart. It makes me ask myself if any preacher is worthy to preach the funeral of any child. It can be done only with a bit of adult presumption and the pretense of a purity we bartered away in the simple process of maturing.

That day I read a childhood scripture, and someone sang Brahms's "Lullaby." I preached to a rather large crowd of what seemed to me a gathering of very bewildered people. I didn't get the reasons for the occasion. They didn't either. It seemed in some ways they had purchased tickets to hear my explanation of some great cosmic riddle. Although I believed God held the ultimate resolution to the puzzle, I was as confused about the reason for your leaving as they were.

Your father was in the military. He was a kind of high-class aide to some high-ranking officer—an adjutant to a general—so there seemed to me to be so many high-level brass at your service that I couldn't have counted them all without an abacus. I was never in the armed services myself, and the overwhelming number of these military mighty ones befuddled me. Actually, I think they unnerved me. I guess it's a phenomenon among those of us who have been lifelong civilians that we feel a bit sissified in the presence of real warriors.

But they were docile. They didn't throw anything. They listened hard to my eulogy as if to say, *We're experts at war. Now we want some answers from a man who is an expert on death and dying.* I am sure I was somewhat of a disappointment to them. There are no experts on death and dying. Worse than that, as I have said, who is really good enough to preach a funeral like yours, Miffy?

When I am really insecure in the pulpit I tend to preach very short sermons without a lot of authority. I got through the entire memorial service in record time; then came the part I really hated: the press of mourners who passed by your tiny little casket to pay their last respects.

I could think of little more to do than to hug them.

I didn't find it much of a chore to hug the civilians who passed by your silent form. But what was I to do about those generals and the upper brass who were there? Hugging is about all the explanation I have to offer at something so unexplainable as a child's funeral. When every set of eyes is asking why, hugging is my only answer. But was it appropriate for a civilian, a wimpy warrior, to hug a general?

Those modern "warlords" were all sitting on one or two long pews, so I faced a long, long file of confusion—and took what was one of the biggest risks of my ministry. When the first general came by, I grabbed him with vehemence and hugged him. Then, surprise of surprises, he hugged me back. He hugged me hard, like a pentecostal deacon on steroids. He held on for a long time.

There were tears in his eyes, and his whole frame seemed to shudder with grief. Then I knew. There are all kinds of wars. The kind generals fight and the kind nobody understands. We are fellow travelers on the way to the world where you already are, and we all need a little help along our own private yellow-brick road to glory.

I knew too why he held on so long. It wasn't just that he agreed with me that there are no words in the worst of battles. He held on to give hugging permission to all the men who followed him. Gaining courage, I hugged the rest of them.

Even for generals, the best answer to the mystery of death was an embrace. It was the best time I ever had hugging generals.

The service was over. We gathered at your tiny grave, that obscene hole in the earth that seemed too small to suck in all the question marks. I had written a poem that helped me through the required moments. By the time I read it, you had already been in heaven quite a while. It was a little exalted in theme for you to really understand. I suspect I had really written it for all your adult admirers so they could get the picture of a very bright and happy little girl who had just found herself in a crystal playground a world away from where we were forced to reckon with your remains.

In some way it was easier for me to visualize you skipping through heaven than it was to imagine you amid more grandiose heavenly images, cowering among a multitude of angels robed in intimidating splendor. So I offered this sonnet, "To Miffy," as your small, white casket sank slowly into the dark earth:

I've waited till your second day in heaven.
Your first day there would seem to you a treat.
You'd gaze about in wonder at the view
Of all the city gathered in the street.
So many I know here are quite afraid

To face their final fears and cross the sea.

You swam so easily! What courage made

You unafraid to face eternity?

Did God appear a high-rise trinity?

Did glass or tow'ring crystal dazzle you?

Did Christ not cry, "Let this child come to me

And give her room to skip this avenue!"?

At those grand gates which close against the night,

He scooped you up and carried you to light.

NARNIA ON
THE WAY

My little stepdaughter, after she read all

the Narnia stories, cried bitterly, saying,

"I don't want to go on living in this world.

I want to live in Narnia with Aslan."

Darling, one day you will.

——— ◈ ———

George Sayer,
Jack

GEORGE SAYER

We met in 1997 at Regent's Park College in Oxford. I called you on a hunch—one that held no real expectation—to ask if you could come to the college to lecture for a day to a class that I was teaching on C. S. Lewis. Amazingly, you agreed, and the day we spent together I have stored in my memory box as one of the great days of my life.

Before and after class we talked, then lunched, and talked some more. My knowledge of Lewis was average—all the things that can be learned from reading his books and a half-dozen biographies. Your *Life of Lewis* was then, and remains to this day, my favorite of all.

At the time I was there, Richard Attenborough was too. So were Anthony Hopkins and Debra Winger. The whole movie company was there filming *Shadowlands*. I am still not wholly at ease about this particular metaphor that Lewis gave us. *Shadowlands* is us! Narnia is on the way. The difficulty with building a metaphorical heaven is that it often becomes quite fixed, and the real nature of the place is subverted by the poetry of our own imaginations.

Since eternity is a place we haven't been to and also a place from which we cannot return, we must rely on metaphors to give us the only definitions we can have. The pictures of the court of God in the Bible—in books like the Apocalypse of St. John—indicate a grand reality, and yet we get the feeling that the apostle is confronted with painting the same poetic pictures most of us have when we journey into the realm of forever.

Most of the hymns we sang in the church of my youth were poetic metaphors. We sang them lustily, never thinking much of their symbolic character:

The hill of Zion yields a thousand sacred sweets
Before we reach the heavenly fields, or walk the golden
  streets.[1]

To that home on God's celestial shore, I'll fly away.[2]

When his chosen ones shall gather to their home beyond
  the skies,
And the roll is called up yonder I'll be there.[3]

I've reached the land of love divine, and all its riches now are mine. . . . Beulah Land.[4]

Narnia takes all these metaphorical pictures to a new level. The intricacy, the topography, the lion King—and all the descriptions are so fully developed.

Isaiah welcomes us into the love of God, which never forgets that all our metaphors of all things eternal at last must fail. "As the heavens are higher than the earth, so are [God's] ways higher than your ways, and [his] thoughts than your thoughts" (Isaiah 55:9).

Metaphors are but a way of dealing with the grand realities of God that always seem to elude us. They are but weak flashlights turned against the glaring reality of "shadowless lands."

So I must ask you, George: how is it there? You managed to outlive Lewis by forty-two years. You've been in Narnia since October 2005. How do you find it? Do the metaphors hold? I wish you could tell me how close they come, but I suspect they do not come very close. Even metaphors as splendid as Narnia are not so ideal as we thought; they are but a shabby substitute for the real glory of the place that seems to be unfolding in Revelation 4.

I am always reminded of the tale widow of Parker Pillsbury urging his dying friend, Ralph Waldo Emerson, to describe his passing into the next realm.

"What's it like?" insisted Pillsbury.

"One world at a time, Parker, one world at a time," counseled Emerson.

The thing we never get to see in *Shadowlands* is the death of the Pevensie children. In *The Last Battle*, we find that the Pevensies have been dead from the very first of the seventh book. They felt the train lurch, that was all, and suddenly they were in Narnia. But the horrors of the train crash—the instant maiming, the blood, the brokenness of these tiny kings and queens, Peter, Susan, Lucy, and Edmond—were all left behind in the Shadowlands, and suddenly they were with Aslan in his world.

I think most of us have a hard time going from the harsh world of train wrecks and death to "the land that is fairer than day."[5] Lewis, in *A Grief Observed*, indeed seemed to have that same trouble. After his wife Joy's death, he was mad with alienation and confusion and said nothing much of Narnia, which he spent so many years writing of.

I assume, George, that you went on to heaven before your stepdaughter. Remember the exchange. She said upon completing the Narnia books, "I don't want to go on living in this world. I want to live in Narnia with Aslan."

And you said, "Darling, one day you will."

We leave the world where we never were really at home to inherit the one we never have to leave. But this transition is not really a leap into darkness. Instead it is a leap from our metaphorical definitions into the reality we must get comfortable with.

I recently suffered a heart attack. The pain was immense, but what I discovered was that I was utterly at peace with the notion that Narnia came next, and I could possibly be there in the next moment. Contrary to those who talk about near-death in terms of bright lights, dark tunnels, and family reunions, I experienced only the wonder of transcendence. I was extremely happy to let God surprise me with it all. I saw nothing. I lived and experienced the vague but peaceful realm of coronary care.

At that border of life that a man must cross, I was content and eager to know the land that I have described in metaphor, knowing fully that splendor was about to dawn, but in no way knowing the nature of what it would be. I could not guess. I didn't want to guess, for guesses—like metaphors—are only for those who fish in darkness. The reality drew close, and it was wonderful, but it remained undefined.

Did the true nature of Narnia surprise you, George? I suspect it at least overwhelmed you with wonder.

Here's what I learned about metaphors the night of my heart attack: Aslan is key. Really, Aslan is the only key! This Turkish word that bears no etymological similarity to the Greek word *Christos* is the grand point of union. His is the transcendent name, and I shall one day be with him in face-to-face foreverness, whatever this fully means. I know that without Christ, the best heaven would be shabby indeed! I feel sorry for Muslim martyrs who must imagine their heaven only in terms of virgins. What a poor eternity is theirs!

I know that now you are in his presence. I also know you must keep this great reality to yourself. You cannot photograph true reality and send it back to our realm, so we must go on living in anticipation, clinging to our metaphors. But however we imagine it, Narnia is on the way. It is our mansion over the hilltop. It is Beulah land. It is Zion. It is the land that is fairer than day. All these metaphors are places; but real heaven is a Person.

It is Aslan.

It is Christ.

It is union with Christ.

The only anthem I know that transcends all the word pictures we waiting lovers have devised is this:

Face to face with Christ, my Savior,
Face to face—what will it be,
When with rapture I behold him,
Jesus Christ who died for me?[6]

A GRIEF OBSERVED

All their life in this world and all their adventures

in Narnia have only been the cover and the title

page: now at last they were beginning Chapter One

of the Great Story which no one on earth has read.

—— ༄ ——

C. S. Lewis,
The Last Battle

By the time you died in November 1963, I was twenty-seven years old and already well read in all of your works I could get my hands on. I was unaware of your passing on that day because President Kennedy was assassinated on the same day, and his death completely eclipsed your own in the headlines. Nonetheless, I continued to read and study you for the next forty years, and even now I pick up and read your work simply to clear the mud from my thinking.

I have collected all your works—some in the first edition—and have annotated and marked each volume with notes. I have taught Lewis courses in several seminaries, both in America and abroad, but I have never been asked to teach or speak about you in any of the grand, formal venues of international scholarship. So often the programs on those occasions have been put together by denominational groups or evangelical scholars who either don't know me or do not hold me in high enough esteem to ask me to participate.

Still, I feel as though, if I *had* been asked, I could have done so with enough competence to have added something to the program. I have "taught Lewis" for American study programs at Oxford and have thoroughly explored your small, tight world of Magdalen College, Headington Hill, the Kilns, as well as the Cambridge world. I have read all your biographies, both authorized and "un."

I say all this to convince you that, among all those who esteem and understand your life and work, I have at least been fastidious in my effort. None of us achieve all we would like in our attempt to succeed in our own eyes, and you must have gone to your grave in the Trinity churchyard, regretting not having been buried in the crypts of Westminster Abbey as the "national" poet you would have liked. For that matter, you were never elevated to Cecil Day-Lewis's coveted position as the Magdalen College Poet.

Of course there are places where even the greatest of men have some weakness of doctrine. My own esteem for T. S. Eliot is so great that I wanted this same esteem to be yours. Alas, you never cared much for Eliot. But by and large, your work is so incredible that we Western evangelicals see you as nearly infallible in helping us explain ourselves to ourselves.

I read only one of your books with some doubt: *A Grief Observed*. It was written in that three-year interim between Joy's death and your own. It doesn't exactly push God into the chasm of nonexistence, but it is easy to see how it led your critics to say that toward the end of your life you were retreating into the atheism you once escaped to all our benefit. It is not just what you said in that book, but the morose tone of it. It seems in places to be not so much a "grief observed" but one wallowed in and stained by.

When I read it the first time, and each time since, I asked myself, where was that positive tone you achieved in all your other work? Remember when you had the unicorn declare while he feasted his eyes on Aslan's country: "This is the land I have been looking for all my life, though I never knew it until now. The reason that we loved old Narnia is that it sometime looked a little like this."[1]

If ever most of us want some positive picture of heaven and salvation, it is here at the threshold of life. *A Grief Observed* is a short book (perhaps your shortest); perhaps any brightness of mood was compromised by your own deteriorating health.

Catch the mood. Listen to yourself and the dour emptiness you seem to wallow in: you seem to intimate that you are "an unhappy man [who] wants distractions" with God, but in desperation you get to him, "and what do you find? A door slammed in your face."[2] Yet you seem to admit that there's no danger you'll revert to unbelief. "The real danger is of coming to believe such dreadful things about him."[3]

From the inner darkness of your grief, you wrote, "A corpse, a memory, and (in some versions) a ghost. All mockeries or horrors. Three more ways of spelling the word *dead*."[4]

It is this negative sound that makes your God, at the end of your life, seem so not-to-be-counted-on. If it were possible, I would have you tell me that this anger toward death passed, and there was the God who you said was always in the dock, put there by unhappy souls who had things to demand of him.

Is God really a cosmic sadist? Is the only pleasure we can have in the depths of our grief that of hitting God back? You said all reality is *iconoclastic*.[5] Did you really mean that, or was it merely your observed grief giving God a good one in his solar plexus? Did you really mean it—even at the time—when you called God the *Eternal Vivisectionist*?[6]

Somehow, you did better when Joy was sick. Remember? You asked her, if she could, to come to you also when you were on your deathbed. And remember? She said, "Allowed! Heaven would have a job to hold me; and as for Hell, I'd break it into bits!"[7]

It is Joy's muscular optimism that I wish permeated your testament of grief.

The Bible is replete with joy and victory on the subject of the believer's entrance into heaven. Remember what you said about it in *The Great Divorce*? "Heaven is not a state of mind, Heaven is reality itself!"[8]

Anyway, I am sure that when we finally meet in heaven, I will be somewhere near the back of the long line of all those who have waited their entire lives to meet you. There must be a half-billion disciples whom you have tutored in the living, dying faith. Maybe there, in better light, you will display the customary optimism about God that so marked your life. In the meantime, I wait for our first conversation when I will be washed with a steadfast credulity, and you will have fully recovered your joyous, eternal optimism.

TO A GODLY MAN WITH A MAD WIFE

There was a mad man and he had a mad wife,

And they lived in a mad town:

And they had children three at a birth,

And mad they were every one.

The father was mad and the mother was mad,

And the children mad beside.

And they all got on a mad horse,

And madly they did ride.

They rode by night and they rode by day,

Yet never a one of them fell:

They rode so madly all the way,

Till they came to the gates of hell.

Old Nick was glad to see them so mad,

And gladly let them in:

But he soon grew sorry to see them so merry,

And let them out again.

—— ⦿〰〰〰⦿ ——

Old English nursery rhyme

GOOD JOHN SMITHSON

John, now that you're in heaven, and I am yet to arrive, is it okay that I tell you I never much liked your wife? I'm sure—at least reasonably so—that you and Sophie are back together again, and that Sophie made it through the gates with only a minor check of her credentials. If Sophie was a saint, she was certainly—as Teresa of Avila might have said—a frowning saint.

Teresa of Avila was not fond of sourpuss Christians and actually said on another occasion, "I won't have nuns who are ninnies" (however you say that in Spanish or Latin).

Everyone who knew both of you realized that all of Sophie's minuses were sanctified by your pluses. I never saw you look cross at her when she seemed to be able to look no other way. I will always believe you were the avatar of Saint Joseph, the patron saint of married men.

You were handsome, winsome, jovial. Your eyes were the very expression of kindness. You opened car doors for her when you arrived at church. You carried her Bible into the house of God. I wondered if she had ever read it. I know you did. It even seemed to most of us that you could have written it.

Which of the martyrs said, "Joy is the most infallible proof of the presence of God"? Whoever it was had you in mind. You preceded Sophie into heaven, and what a well-earned respite for you!

I don't know if Sophie ever told you that she came to my office to relate to me the "shortcomings" of some of those "other Christians" who belonged to our church. It amazed me that she could see so many of the faults that were obvious in other people's lives but so few of her own.

I know you never knew this, John, but she kept a little book on me, her pastor. One day she called me on the phone while I was deep in study at church. She spoke rather sharply into the receiver, "Pastor, if you don't get over to my house right now, I am going to scuh . . . *ream!*"

I was a much younger pastor then, and Sophie actually frightened me. So I ran as fast as I could and jumped into my car and headed over to your house. I've grown more mature since those days, and if that were to happen today, I would not run to respond quite so quickly. Now I would stop for coffee and loiter along the way. But, as I said, in those days I was terrified of Sophie, and so I answered her summons as quickly as I could.

She met me at the door. "Pastor, come in here!"

I managed to say, "Hello there! How's it going, Sophie?"

"Not well," she said, "but I don't want to talk about me. I want to talk about you. You may not be aware of this, but I've got a little black notebook, here." She waved a tiny black notebook in my face as she went on. "And I've been writing down everything you have done as a 'man of God' that is not in the Spirit of Christ!" And then she said, "Take a chair, pastor; I want to read it to you!"

She began to read a rather extended list of my pastoral sins. There were quite a lot of them; so many, in fact, that I was amazed that they could all be written down in such a little book.

Sophie obviously wrote with a stingy little hand. The devil's letters never need a generous alphabet.

What amazed me, John, was how many things I actually *had* done that were not in the Spirit of Christ. I felt like I was before that Great Accounting, being read to from the big book described in Revelation 20:12. I can understand why the earth and sea fled away from that book. It was horrible.

My sins were many, and I made a vow right there not to sin so much in the future. About the only sin I hadn't done was to keep a little book on Sophie.

After that reading, we were destined not to be good

friends, but still I tried to be on my best behavior and not sin so much, at least not right out in the open whenever Sophie had her little book with her.

When I told my wife about Sophie's little book, she asked me, "Do you think she keeps a little book on John?"

It made me wonder. I don't know if she had a book-keeping system on everybody, but if so, I can understand how her iniquity research must have fatigued her spirit. Maybe that's why she never smiled much. I don't know. I only know she didn't. She loved hymns, and that seemed almost irreconcilable with her continual, sour-puss expression.

I remember seeing her driving her car once at the corner of 132nd and Center Streets. While I waited for the light to change so I could take my turn at the intersection, Sophie zoomed through at the last second of an amber light. Her face was aimed straight ahead, and I wondered if she was listening to hymns on a Christian radio station.

I believe in shooting prayers at other believers when I am not able to actually talk to them. So I shot a prayer at Sophie. Some prayers are destined to be ignored, I guess, and I noticed no change in her mood. Then she was gone. The light flashed a welcome green, and I traveled on my way.

Jesus once said, "When the dead rise, they will neither marry nor be given in marriage; they will be like the angels in heaven" (Mark 12:25 NIV). Angels don't get married, said Jesus, and neither will mortals once they change estates. I have never liked this particular truth myself. To be suddenly unmarried to my dear Barbara is not much of an incentive for me to even want to go there.

But then I thought of you, John. Patient, kind, gracious, winsome—hardly the kind of man whom anyone could keep an evil account of. And I wondered, once you went to heaven, if the Christ you served as the joy of your life didn't welcome you in with a grand hallelujah and a pat on the back. But then, after Sophie joined you and she was given her glorified body and its new, angelic countenance, could you actually recognize her?

When I get to heaven, I want to join the both of you, and though I may approach Sophie with a cautious respect—having known her in her earthly life—I want to see what she looks like in her new, beatific state. The great thing about this coming reunion is that I know what you will look like, John: you will look like the saint you rehearsed becoming all your life.

The man you will be was the man you were.

What a role model for all Christian husbands. When you said, "for better, for worse, forever . . . ," you weren't kidding around.

DYING AT A FORK IN THE ROAD

We rest on Thee, our Shield and our Defender,

Thine is the battle, Thine shall be the praise,

When passing through the gates of pearly splendor,

Victors, we rest with Thee through endless days.

—— ୧୦୦୦ ——

"We Rest on Thee,"

The last hymn sung by missionary Jim Elliot,

January 8, 1956

W e never met. You were born nine years before me. Yet I felt I must include you in my letters to heaven. When I graduated from college in 1958, *The Shadow of the Almighty* had just been published by your young widow, and the weight of its import fell upon my confused life like a bomb of clarity.

I was a student pastor at the time. At age nineteen I had become pastor of a small Baptist church with a robust attendance of around seventy in Hunter, Oklahoma. While I was way over my head in my ability to practice "the cure of souls," I wanted with every fiber of my being to please Christ in my commitment to his kingdom. But there was something superficial in it all.

I never really understood this superficiality until I learned of your own passion for the pleasure of God's approval. You were thirty-one when I was twenty-two. In you I came face-to-face with the man who wrote:

> Father, make of me a crisis man. Bring those I contact to decision. Let me not be a mile post on a single road; make me a fork, that men must turn one way or another on facing Christ in me.[1]

I was in a rural church but contemplating a move to the city. What city? *Some* city! And when I got there, I wanted to care about that city the way you seemed to care about all cities. When I read this statement from your journal, I wanted to be a "fork in the road," but I realized there were a couple of different forks that were trying to claim my desire.

There was the fork I would become that forced all men to see the Christ in me and decide which fork they would take. But I realized I needed to take a fork of my own—the one Robert Frost wrote of, where choosing the "road less traveled . . . made all the difference."[2]

I can only imagine that those wonderful things you wrote in your journal have been counsel to a lot of lives like mine. But eight years after I read your words, I found myself in a northern city: Omaha, Nebraska. I suppose it was "north" to me since I grew up far south of there and attended a university in Oklahoma. I wanted to plant a church, and such a calling always elicits a will that is tough enough for the job.

I've tried to imagine that day you died on the Curaray River in Ecuador. You wanted to be a fork that called men to decide a way. And though they didn't on that day, in time . . . in time . . . in time, they did.

Then, ten years after your ultimate sacrifice, I accepted your mandate as my own and decided I too would be a fork in the road. It was odd that your lonely jungle death would speak to me then—and on into the rest of my life. But it did. It was hard to measure the moment, for it seemed even to me a small thing. I was going to the city to plant a church. It was not a large city as urban centers go, but several hundred thousand people even so. And you had been in the jungle with a handful of naked savages because they had not heard and could neither read nor write the language you had grown so wonderfully efficient at.

We had a Baptist professor who made light of your death for so few. "Why," he asked, "would Mr. Elliot give his life for such a few savages when he might have won so many just miles away in Quito, without facing danger? His death was simply not good stewardship. Arrow-through-the-neck missions is a poor economy, given to an inefficient handful while it ignores the millions of lost in the vast cities of the world."

There were probably others who criticized you this way. But your nobility of spirit survived the caustic criticism. It always does: real sacrifice ever outlives its critics.

By that time I knew you, Mr. Elliot. I had felt your passion. I knew the truth: we never love populations, only people. The best of us who want to be forks in the road are driven mad by the passion God places in our lives.

Fork people are possessed by a magnificent obsession to please God. So they live at the fork for the sake of the undecided whom God has put on their hearts. As Robert Frost concluded, it was that choice that has "made all the difference"—for you, for me.

I determined that if hell and heaven were real, then that choice must be the ultimate fork in the road. So I would give my life to the winning of men and women to Christ. It was a formative decision. Hell was forever. So was heaven. The stakes, therefore, were ultimate.

I confronted my new city with some bewilderment. How would I start? Where would I start? There were so many who stood at the fork, yet I did not know a single name. And that's where I began, with names. I subscribed to a little paper called the *Daily Record.* It was an odd little flyer that listed the legal stuff that had happened in our city on any given day: divorces, foreclosures, litigations, trials—all the stuff that made for human misery. It also listed all the newcomers to our city, by address. In short, it was a little tabloid of names and addresses, and in some cases, it told something of their woes.

I began to call on the people named in the *Daily Record*. They fit my fork-in-the-road mentality. They had names, and names were all I needed. In those days, pastors called on needy people, so most people didn't ask me how I got their names or learned of their needs. And within a few moments in most situations, we were talking freely and comfortably. Then, somewhere in all the camaraderie, I spoke to them about Christ, and in many cases they were eager to know how he could help. Within a few years, a church was born, and within twenty-five years it had three thousand people in its membership.

So, Jim, your entrance into heaven was most timely. I cannot say that if you had not died so young, your Betty would ever have written of your life. But your home-going was just in the nick of time for me. My whole life was redeemed by your counsel, and the fork of the road I tended was a place of decision for thousands.

I owe you much. And, by the way, you were entirely correct about the decisive life when you said, "He really is no fool who gives what he cannot keep to gain what he cannot lose."

All fork-in-the-road people know this.

DO DEAD MEN STILL WALK THE EARTH?

Some ten thousand persons . . . were singing hymns.
. . . Then I "saw" him, my father who had died long
before at age eighty-five. He came striding down the
aisle . . . about forty years old. . . . I was spellbound
. . . [by] what I was "seeing."

———— ✦ ————

Norman Vincent Peale

We were never close, but I must confess I felt a cama-raderie with you on three separate occasions. The first two of these moments came when my family and I visited your church, Marble Collegiate Church in New York. My children were fascinated by the box pews of the old church and the usher who shut all four of us into one box and then closed the gate. It was a nuance in worship for them (and for me as well), and they never ceased talking about it.

I was fascinated by the open style of your chancel, and while you wore a robe when you preached, it was the openness of your stance that intrigued me. You stood all alone with no pulpit between you and the people—just you, the Word of God, and oxygen—and you talked to all of us in a conversational voice rich in texture and full of wisdom.

I knew that the word *homily*, from which we derive the word *homiletics*, meant "conversation," but having been a lifelong Baptist, a denomination in which passion—often akin to much shouting—is the definition of the "homiletical style," I was spellbound by the notion of persuasion minus pulpit thumping. Those two visits led me to my own style of conversational persuasion.

On my end of Christianity—a highly conservative and fundamentalist end—there were many who were critical of you. To them your positivist pulpit bore in it a great deal of heresy. "It is too little Bible and too much Norman," they said, totally blind to the coming shape of things. It may have seemed so during the final decades of the twentieth century. But in the present decade, the megachurch has so weakened biblical preaching that your sermons, it seems now to me, were always quite biblical by comparison.

Many said you should have quoted Saint Paul more and your own worldview a little less, which led ultimately to the cliché, "Paul is appealing but Peale is appalling." I teach preaching now and have ordered the sermons of many megachurch pastors for a library that students can dip into as they seek to build their own preaching style. Yet often I have sent back the ordered recordings and transcripts because I don't want my students to preach Scripture-less sermons. However, I can never recall hearing one of your sermons that didn't at least mention a scripture and then proceed from that scripture to a sound homily challenging us all to move to a Christ-centered base for building our worldview.

You were sometimes labeled an occultist, for some dark reasons I cannot fathom. It all seemed to go back to one particular incident. In 1984, you were preaching to a large congregation of thousands. During the exuberant song service that preceded your sermon, you saw your father, who had, at that time, been with the Lord for many years, having died in his mid-eighties. You saw him coming down the aisle, youthful once again—in his mid-forties—bright and warm and very much alive. Those who were at the meeting saw you advance to the edge of the stage and reach out to receive him, when he disappeared and was gone. All who were there noticed your behavior and were stunned by it.

At the time I thought little of it and would have let it lie silent as a moment of inspiration brought on by the joyful singing of the group. To me it was like a fleeting vision given you to affirm his place in heaven and to be enshrined in your own private remembrance of him as well. But my understanding of it was not yours.

As I recall, you came to Omaha at about that same time to speak at a Chamber of Commerce convention or some such gathering. I was the pastor of a large church in the city then, and was asked by the program committee to say the invocation at the luncheon at which you were the keynote speaker. In some ways it was a notable time in my own life because I was in the next-to-last chair at the table, and you were in the very last chair. This meant that for the better part of an hour, you were held captive between me, with my inquisitive nature, and the end of the table. You had no one to talk to but me, and I relished the opportunity.

I told you of my previous visits to Marble Collegiate Church and the great things you inadvertently taught me about effective pulpit communication. The conversation rolled on, and I shared with you my lifelong admiration for your ministry. In your *Foundation for Christian Living* newsletter, you also had once written a brief review of my first book, *Once Upon a Tree*—a book of sermons I had written for the Lenten season—and you said it was one of the best books on the cross you'd ever read. I felt like a million bucks because of your wonderful affirmation.

It was thrilling for me at this businessmen's luncheon to have this nearly private time with you, and things were going swimmingly until I said, "Tell me about the time you thought you saw your dead father at the camp meeting."

"*Think* I saw him!" you fairly blurted out. "I didn't *think* I saw him. I *saw* him!"

I meant no disrespect and was taken aback that you were taken aback. I realized, after I thought it all through, that your answer on the issue had probably run into a lot of incredulity by this time, and you no doubt felt you had to put down the rumors that were circulating about your supposed indulgence in the occult.

It did seem to me that you took a lot of heat for claiming to have seen your father. The late J. B. Phillips saw C. S. Lewis in his TV room, and he was not chided nearly as much as you. But some of your critics seemed to hound you in the streets.

The Bible is not totally without corroboration in the matter. Moses and Elijah do appear with Jesus in the transfiguration experience. The shape of Samuel also is summoned back from the dead by the witch of Endor. The godly dead walked about the streets of Jerusalem when Jesus died. So I suppose your dead father . . . well, the infraction is not totally without some biblical precedence. But I have never forgotten the vehemence of your reply.

Since Don Piper has now sold millions of books about his temporary visit to heaven, maybe evangelicals these days would be prone to cut you a little more slack. In the meantime, when we're together at last in heaven and there isn't so much money riding on your reputation, maybe we could have a little meeting. Just the three of us: your father, yourself, and me. (Of course, this would all come after we had each greeted our own families, along with Jesus and the patriarchs.) There, with the better light of heaven, we should be able to work out whether the universe next door can—at wonderful, unexpected moments—break in upon our dull days with a kind of glory that only God can explain.

TO A GIRL IN AN IRON LUNG

It seems to be the mission of some in this world

to give and not receive. They are to shine

in the darkness, burning up their own lives

as the lamp's oil burns, to be light to other

souls. . . . We are apt to pity such persons; but

couldn't it be that they are nearer the heavenly

ideal of doing God's will than are some of

those who sit in the sunshine of love, receiving,

ministered unto, but not giving or serving?

———— ⌒᠁〇 ————

J. R. Miller,
The Building of Character

A HERO
WHOSE NAME IS
WITHHELD

You were not the only person I ever knew who had polio. But you were the first person ever to accost me with the logic that the disease was no respecter of persons. Anyone . . . everyone was a potential victim.

Infantile paralysis: that's what we once called polio in rural Oklahoma. Maybe that's what people everywhere called it; I don't know. I only know it was an odd disease. There weren't any rules about how a person got it or how it originated. It wasn't an airborne illness, though so much public superstition thought it was. It was transmitted mostly by direct contact with bodily fluids or by fecal contamination.

I knew another student who had the disease—like yourself, a beautiful young girl. And her own struggles, like yours, were horrible; polio was a killing crippler of the young. I never saw her during the days that she most wrestled with the disease. Only when she came back to school, walking with the greatest of effort, did I know that our mothers were not warning us to steer clear of the disease without cause.

My schoolmate's experience made us all afraid.

And the demon wasn't just for children to conquer. We all knew that President Roosevelt had it. We did not generally know at first that our president was a paraplegic. He rarely allowed himself to be photographed walking or even in a standing position. He came down with the disease in 1921; he was thirty-nine when he contracted it. That caused even greater national fear. Now we knew that no one was immune. Old people and even presidents could battle the contagion—and lose.

Then came the summer you came to town. You arrived in a big semi-trailer inside a white cylindrical tube with a Plexiglas window. The armor shielded you from all kinds of colds and viruses that could further threaten your already tenuous life.

Everyone was talking about your arrival. "Have you gone to see the girl in the iron lung?" they asked each other as they passed one another on the streets.

"What a shame!" they commiserated.

Some few wouldn't go anywhere near the truck that day, just in case the contagion passed through the steel tube and infected their own small-town fears with death. Most passed you, looking down or to the side, avoiding any direct look into your eyes. Sometimes you slept, or appeared to. You didn't speak, and we didn't say hello. You were a huge curiosity point in our newsless, small-time world.

It was your sole intention, I guess, to promote polio awareness. For most of us, you were the living-dead person we all cried for but avoided, fearing that even to care about you would somehow reinforce the notion that your quality of life might become ours. You were the person we vowed never to think of again. You were the surrogate victim in a truck who would leave our town and leave us to think better of ourselves once you moved on to your next destination.

Your truck, wheel-blocked for your stay in front of the courthouse, was welcome mostly because we knew you were on a kind of sideshow tour of America. Your job was to lie quietly in your glass-and-steel reliquary. You could blink, but no other part of your body moved, and your blinking was the only way you could tell us that you were a human being too.

Besides the blinking, it was the iron lung that drove you into our awareness. There was only the rasping swish of air in and out of your lungs created by the powerful bellows of your large machine. It's ironic how such a mechanism caused all of us to be aware of the sound of our own breath, the sheer human romance of trading oxygen for CO_2. I listened for my own breath, blinked, and thanked God. But for what? I thanked him that I was not like you. That's what mothers told their children: "When you say your nighty-night prayers, you thank God you're not like the girl in the iron lung."

I can't remember if the touring iron lung was a part of the national call to polio awareness or the severity of infantile paralysis. Perhaps it was sponsored by the March of Dimes, the president's charge to every American to give a single dime to help rid the world of polio. The U.S. citizenry responded to President Roosevelt's call by ultimately putting his picture on every dime minted by the U.S. Treasury. Each time I gave a dime, my friend, I thought of you. I wanted to give, and I wanted you to be out of that horrible truck.

Sometimes I would encounter the crippled girl in our school who had wrestled with polio and had done better than you did in your struggle. Still, her braced legs and her crutches reminded me of your plight—and conjured up the same fears. When I would see her in the hall, I wanted to take another route to get to my class. But in the oddest sort of way, she was the one who caused me to finally conquer my fears. Gradually the demon was exorcised. Gradually the taboo lifted.

I remember the first real conversation I ever had with

her. She assured me I couldn't get polio just by talking to those who had it. One day she and I had a good conversation, and before long, my fears were gone. I remember thinking, *Gosh, old chum, you are just like I am.* Polio victims were not lepers who needed to be hidden away. They were people with the same need to relate to others as me.

Years later I met a beautiful woman named Anne. Her leg was braced too. I heard she was a polio survivor; in time she became our church pianist. She was vivacious and wonderful.

Once I had come to know her well, I asked her how she had gotten polio, and she quietly told me her life story. She said that in her late teens she had become very proficient at playing the piano—so much so that her parents were making tentative plans for her to enter Juilliard or one of the other great American conservatories. Then came polio! She knew the devastation of the disease and made a bargain with God that if he would let her survive the plague with both of her hands and one good foot to run the pedals, then she would abandon her dream of being a famous concert artist and give her life to the church, using her talent for God.

When the disease had passed, she had lost the use of one of her legs, but the other was fine. And her hands . . . well, by the time I came to know her, they had thrilled every audience that heard her play. With her testimony fortifying me, I at long last made a truce with my fears, and the demons of childhood never possessed me again.

But it was you, my nameless instructor in an iron lung, who really taught me courage. In you I came to see that any monster, no matter its fangs, can be beaten in time. It can be beaten with good resolve and by running toward the beast until you can see it close enough.

I am sorry that I treated you with such avoidance that day I passed you in your truck. You no doubt noticed.

Your paralysis must be a testament that all of us are crippled in some sense. I certainly was. Terribly misshapened in my mind and terribly misshapened in my conduct toward you. And so I am shortly to join you in heaven, where every pair of legs is straight and every quadriplegic is an acrobat, and where, best of all, every intolerance has been washed in grace. You have already been made perfect in that bright sphere. And I shortly will be.

Lord Byron was off and on an agnostic, but in his better moments he owned up to the fact that the idea of renewal in paradise at least appealed to him. Elizabeth Longford says that Byron's bitterness over his own crippled condition is reflected in his words, "And our carcasses, which are to rise again, are they worth raising? I hope, if mine is, that I shall have a better pair of legs than I have moved on these two-and-twenty years, or I shall be sadly behind in the squeeze into paradise."[1]

It really is true that they also serve who only stand and wait—or, in your case, blink! Because breathing is better in a place where praise is so customary, and where blinking is replaced by running and leaping to God's good glory, we don't give much thought to breathing or our freedom to move. We will have been there a thousand years before it suddenly occurs to us: *I haven't seen a cripple in a millennium.*

And those old white semi-trailers once used for exhibitionist sideshows? They're all rusting away in hell now.

Once in heaven, we will see things for what they are. Polio in eternity's better light is just the healing opportunity of God. So I await our coming together. Be careful! You may not recognize me right off. Thanks to you, I have been cleansed of most of my self-righteousness.

SCORE: GOD ONE, CANCER ZERO

Hearts on earth say in the course

of a joyful experience,

"I don't want this ever to end." But

it invariably does.

The hearts of those in heaven say,

"I want this to go on forever."

And it will. There can be no better news than this.

—— ∾☽∾ ——

J. I. Packer

ORMOND BENTLEY

In your last valiant weeks of life, a very good friend of yours spoke my sentiment exactly when he said, tongue-in-cheek, "I'd sure hate to be a cancer and have to fight it out with you."

I knew what he meant. You fought the Grim Reaper so magnificently that, often, those of us who held front-row seats for the bout didn't see the real enemy. Your smile, your easy laughter, your quick wit, your love of a good argument—all these accoutrements of courage were your garments of congeniality that kept us from seeing the dragon that roared against you.

But we knew.

Mary, your wife of half a century, knew too. I watched her loving you, as she always had. I could see her heart breaking when we sat at lunch in the hospital cafeteria.

We both constantly urged you to eat. I remember practically forcing you to drink a milkshake at a fast-food franchise. I knew how disgusting the thing was to you, and yet you drank it, if only to appease my determination to keep you alive.

I knew in you that rare and chaste rapport that can exist between same-gender friends. I was fortunate to know the force of what David said of Jonathan after the battle of Mount Gilboa: "I grieve for you, Jonathan, my brother; you were very dear to me. Your love for me was wonderful, more wonderful than that of women" (2 Samuel 1:26 NIV).

Now, needless to say, I miss you.

But I also realize that, as Jesus said in his parable of the rich man and the beggar, between eternity and this moment there is "a great chasm," so that those who want to return from heaven cannot. Nor can those who want to leave this life and sally into heaven find such a journey possible while they live (Luke 16:26). We were only two years apart in age, my friend, but close enough in time that the heaven you gained will be mine as well, and soon. There were things we talked about that I do wish we had finished. I wish we had talked more thoroughly about death and dying.

Death, said Hamlet, is that "undiscover'd country" from whose "bourn no traveller returns."[1] I would have smuggled a camera into your velvet-lined casket if you could have photographed all you now see and emailed the images back to me. But heaven is like a Broadway play: no photography is permitted.

When you were so ill and your cancer stood lurking about, threatening your existence, we spoke of heaven and of those books so popular in our day, books written by those who went there to visit for a while—minutes in some cases—and then came back. In Jesus' story, the rich man, uncompassionate to the poor scoundrel who begged at his gate, didn't go to heaven but to hell. Yet the rules were the same. There was a great chasm, said the Savior, between the living and the dead, and those who leave the world of the living can never return (Luke 16:19–31).

Dear separated friend, was Jesus right? I've never known him to be otherwise, but what about that uncrossable chasm between the living and the dead? Is it there? Is it uncrossable? Can we go there in near-death experiences? So many see the long, dark tunnel and the light at the end of it, and in most every case the light turns out to be Jesus. The metaphor is splendid, but it is given to us by those innumerable folk who managed to turn their back on the light and then reverse their trek through the tunnel.

Those who linger at the end of the tunnel for a few minutes before they return tell us of what they saw: their dear mother in her gilded rocker, singing "Amazing

Grace." Their granny in her old flannel robe, reading her tear-stained Bible. Their nephew who perished in a hunting accident. Their mate of long-lost anniversaries. Some few mention seeing Jesus, but he is usually indistinct, as in a cloud of light. In nineteenth-century séances, dearly departed friends came back with table rappings and told the living of the location of Auntie's lost pearl brooch or the final cache of her love letters, so long hidden.

There is only one such story in the Bible that I know of, told in 1 Samuel 28; it describes Saul consulting with a medium. "What do you see?" asked Saul.

"I see a spirit coming up out of the ground."

"What does he look like?"

"An old man wearing a robe," said the medium.

Hearing this description, Saul knew at once that it was the dead prophet Samuel, and he prostrated himself with his face to the ground. Then Samuel, a bit enraged that he had been awakened out of Sheol, said, "Why have you disturbed me by bringing me up?"

Saul had gone to the medium in disguise to seek a happy little prediction from Samuel about how his coming battle with the Philistines would go. Alas, the prophet had no good word for the nervous king. "The Lord has torn your kingdom out of your hands," Samuel told Saul. Then he added the news that Saul would soon join him in eternity: "Tomorrow you and your sons will be with me" (NIV).

It wasn't a good word that Saul got, and overall the Scriptures seem to look with disfavor on séances by any name.

On the Mount of Transfiguration, Elijah and Moses both appear and enter into discourse with Jesus (Matthew 17:1–13). But that was not really a spooky return since Elijah was already bodily in heaven (2 Kings 2:11) and Moses, after dying on Mount Nebo, was in heaven as well (Deuteronomy 32:48–52; Jude 9), or so it was believed. Then too, when Jesus breathed his last on the cross, the bodies of many holy people came up out of their graves in an eerie display of God's power over all death (Matthew 27:51–53). But there seemed to be nothing of tunnels and lights in these very few mentions of the dead coming alive again.

The way evangelicals go to heaven and come back seems most intriguing. Their description of heaven is, for me, far too rooted in earthly images. Seeing Grandma and Uncle Harry doesn't necessarily degrade the image; it just makes it almost too "homey" to believe. Those are the kinds of images we sang about in songs such as "Lord, Build Me a Cabin in the Corner of Gloryland" (a too-folksy view of the anticipated celestial palaces of Zion, it seems to me) and "I've Got a Mansion Just over the Hilltop" (maybe, but claiming this ethereal real estate is not the best credential for getting into heaven), and "Tell Mother I'll Be There" (Mother probably knows). This is the countryish and romantic heaven evangelicals usually seem to visit.

Ormond, I knew you well enough to know we both wanted to go to heaven *to see Jesus.* He is, after all, the longed-for One during true believers' sojourn here. Are there streets of gold and gates of pearl? I don't object to the image; it is biblical. But, for my part, there is an ache in my heart, not for the grandeur of upscale real estate, but to be in the company of Christ. If Grandma and Uncle Harry are there, it's because they lived and served this longing.

These come-and-go visitors to heaven have seen too much, but they've seen it with earthly eyes. And what did they hear? Some, like one child who went and returned, heard angels singing. Do angels sing? We all believe they do . . . and play harps too. But the Bible never says they sing. All those angels over the Judean hillside on the night Jesus was born? The Bible says they spoke to the shepherds and glorified God, but it never says they *sang.*

Having seen things as they are, you know on your side of the divide—as I know on mine—that the miracle of Christ's resurrection is that he actually did it. That is why the resurrection is the queen of all miracles. The chasm has been crossed, and Hebrews 12:2 calls Jesus the "author" (NKJV) and "perfecter" (NIV) of our faith.

The word *perfecter* is a Greek word full of image. It is the word *archegos,* which has often been translated as "pioneer," a literal "first-goer" across the fearsome chasm. And to date he is not just the "first" goer but the "only" goer.

So Hamlet was wrong! There *is* an exit bridge from hell, and Jesus found it. The Apostles' Creed says he descended into hell before he left Calvary's chamber of horror and then ascended to "the right hand of the Father." He found his way out of Hamlet's "undiscover'd country" from which no traveler returns to say, "There is a way, and I have done it."

You were a true disciple, Ormond. I have no doubts that you now are so completely absorbed in that indefinable glory that occupies your joy that you have no real desire to return to this shabby land and sing about the homey stuff of our pitiful view of heaven. I know well what you would say if you could take a hasty U-turn out of heaven.

You would say, "Nothin' doin'! I'm staying right here in this glorious place you poor earthlings have yet to encounter and never could imagine. But what I would like to say is, take heart, all cancer victims and those who now swelter under a sheet of pain. There is a place of glorious health beyond the pain. And all you have to do to get here is to give up oxygen and pulse. And with the surrender of those poor habiliments will also go tear ducts and terror. Don't be afraid. And know this: you can't come back from here. But that's all right. No one here wants to."

THE VERY STUFF
OF HEAVEN

I thought how she loved pretty things.

And I remembered

she wouldn't need them in heaven.

——— ⟿ ———

Emilie Griffin,
"Remembering Lucy Powell Russell"

BRITTANY
GILSON

They didn't open your casket at the funeral. The fire was too bad, they said. I used to pass your house often on the way to sweep wheat off the railroad tracks that serviced the Salina grain elevator. (I don't know why they called it the *Salina* elevator. It was nowhere near Salina, which was way north in Kansas, hundreds of miles from our Oklahoma town.) Your house seemed almost as small as the scale house that weighed the wheat trucks that went in and out of that towering elevator. It sat like a dilapidated, bungalow orphan at the foot of the soaring concrete grain bins.

I always thought of you as a kind of Jane Eyre. You were not an orphan, as she was, but you were strangely quiet—so quiet that I wondered where your silence came from. (Did you have to learn the art, like we who are more talkative must first learn the art of being noisy?) Therefore we were not friends, but once in the fifth grade, I caught a moment when I saw you across the heads of my peers, and I thought I could see a smile there. It was an odd smile of affirmation that said we should meet. Maybe we could open our lunchboxes and see how our mothers made our egg sandwiches. Mine were scrambled, but Harry Earl's mother fried his eggs over hard.

Instead, you and I ate alone. Besides, if a boy ate with a girl, classmates called him a "sissy." I couldn't risk that, so we never got to eat together. We never sampled the flavor of the homemade jam that stained our thin, white slices of bread from the inside clear through to the outside.

Your smile. I remember it so well. In Mrs. Page's fifth-grade class, we had a geography test in the form of a make-believe radio quiz show. Mrs. Page held up a crisp dollar bill and said it would be the grand prize for anyone who could name the five Great Lakes. Eagerly my hand shot up and, beginning with Lake Superior, I advanced my way, lake by lake, till I reached Ontario.

The dollar was mine! And then, across the heads of thirty other fifth graders, I saw you smiling, and for the first time, I really believed that if all of our less intelligent comrades could be erased, you and I would meet. We would talk about the Great Lakes and the great rivers and all the geography we longed to know about. And best of all, we would be friends.

Then came the fire. We all heard the sirens. We all went and stood afar off and watched the flames rising ghost-like against the white concrete storage bins of the elevator. Smoke was belching from the windows. There were no fire hydrants in that part of the city to service the small, city fire trucks, so there was no way to fight the flames.

On they roared.

Your parents and siblings all made it outside, and your mother despaired as she reached toward the inferno where she knew you were dying. In the cold days that followed, your house sat like a charred tomb.

Some Christians I knew said it was too bad your parents never took you to church. The summation of all those in the pentecostal congregation I attended was that if you didn't go to church, you probably went to hell when you died and how horrible it was, not only to die in a fire, but to spend an eternity in even more fire.

It was the first time I wanted to doubt Christian theology.

Once during those days, our little church hosted a pentecostal evangelist who said that if you wanted to know what hell was like, you had but to stick your finger in the flame of a kerosene lamp and hold it there . . . and hold it there . . . until the pain made you scream, and then "just imagine that flame all over your body forever, 'where their worm dieth not and the fire is not quenched'!" (Mark 9:44 KJV).

I've never liked that sizzling-worm image of hell that so many Baptist evangelists used to frighten us into the asbestos arms of Jesus. So I cried for you that day, Brittany Gilson. I cried not because I thought you were burning in hell but because the heartless church people said you deserved what you got because you skipped Sunday school. I wanted them to see you—the quiet smile, the person who could wish me well because I knew the names of all the Great Lakes. I cried for you because you never got the chance to finish Woodrow Wilson Grade School.

I really didn't believe you were in hell. I didn't think so because I believe that someone with your ability to bless the world with your quiet shyness must surely know Jesus. I have always suspected it's the loud and boisterous who really don't know Jesus, or at least not very well. Somehow, it seems to me, there must be an inverse relationship between being a loudmouth and forcing your way into the peaceable kingdom once your noisy earthly sojourn is over.

There's a little game I play that helps me get to the bottom line of all theology. It's the game of "If I Were God." About any human issue I cannot resolve, I say, "If I were God, would I . . . ?" I'm not trying to be bigoted in always imagining that God would take my course of action; it's just that the game helps me figure out the world.

I think the first time I played "If I Were God" was after

your funeral. I thought, *If I were God, would I send this poor child who suffocated in the fire to hell so she would have to endure an eternity of more of the same?* You helped me to understand that if I were God, I would not have done it, and thus the issue was resolved—God would not have done it either. In my thinking, you went from your little house by the huge elevator directly to heaven. It was not a huge step for you, Brittany Gilson. Your very spirit is the stuff of heaven, I think.

I didn't learn this till a long time later, but at the same time you died, a girl only a little bit older than you was arrested in Amsterdam. In her famous diary she wrote, "I want to go on living even after I die."

The Germans rooted her family out of its hiding place and sent them off to die. Six million others of her noble race perished in a similar way. This girl died a teenage martyr to her radiant spirit. In her last weeks of life with her father, Otto Frank, he said to her, "Always remember this, Anna, there are no walls, no bolts, no locks that anyone can put on your mind."[1]

And so, my dear, lost classmate of so long ago, you are free, in a place that is void of fire and peril. I'm sure you are there and that the stingy Christians who were so ungenerous with their evaluation of you were wrong. I know it. You told me with your eyes the day I named the five Great Lakes.

TO A MAN
WHO DIED BESIDE ME
ON A FLIGHT

Life is an escalator, and there is no way off

except at the end. The only choice is

between directions: up or down.

———— ∞ ————

Peter J. Kreeft,

Heaven

MR. ACHIEVER, ESQ.

I met you on a stormy night in the New Orleans airport in 1985. We were in one of those commuter lounges where the only place you could get a sandwich—on that night an old, old sandwich—was from the vending machine. We were like passengers holding tickets on a flight to hell. The storm outside was furious; sheets of rain obscured the runway, and the wind blew curtains of water across the glass windows of the waiting area, obliterating our view. When we *could* see out, there was nothing except the white outline of our tiny aircraft that was waiting to take us to Memphis—or to hell, whichever came first.

Six of us were holding tickets. I don't remember all of my emotions, but I do remember two things on my mind that night. I did need to get to Memphis, where I was to speak the next morning at a conference, and I wondered if I would make it in time for my scheduled appearance. The other thing that occupied my mind—and perhaps the minds of all the rest of us—was the wish that the airline would just cancel the flight so we could all go to a hotel and sleep out the storm. We could fly to Memphis the next day.

In this dour mood, you began to talk, the overwhelming odor of liquor on your breath filling the space between us. Maybe we all should have been drinking; looking out the window at the storm, and at that tiny plane we were about to get on, liquor might have helped. Being a Baptist teetotaler myself, storm or not, I faced the torrent without chemical assistance. I could hear the slightest slur in your speech, though otherwise you were most intelligible. Our conversation went something like this:

"Bad night," you said.

"Um . . . ," I acknowledged briefly.

"Did you notice what the stock market did today?" This was an abrupt turn into an uncharted conversation. I couldn't imagine why you had barely introduced the subject of weather and then promptly abandoned it. I could only imagine that you were putting far away the fear of being in a little plane in a broad, dark sky.

"Didn't notice," I replied. "Don't pay much attention to the markets."

"Man, did I take a lickin'," you said, and then you went on, "Lucky for me, I dumped some shaky stuff yesterday, so things are better than they might have been. I got a good broker, and I called him at noon yesterday and by four o'clock in the afternoon, I was out of trouble. I got a great broker, did I mention that?"

"Um . . . ," I said, finding the conversation not much to my liking and unable to think of a good way to get into it.

"I'm sorry," you went on. "I tend to repeat myself sometimes. But I don't see how come you don't pay much attention to the markets. I got myself a big house and a couple of sports cars—Porsche Targa, for one—because I do pay attention. There's a lot of money to be made there, and I have made a lot of it."

"Um . . . ," I said, using my single-syllable response that said I was listening only to be polite.

"My kids sure take me to the cleaners though. Those big eastern universities they want to go to cost me a mint. Between a bad day on Wall Street and a long fall for my children at Princeton, I'm glad I've done as well as I have. Did you ever read Napoleon Hill's *Think and Grow Rich?*"

"Nope," I said.

"You oughta read that."

There was a pause, so I ventured a creative line in place of the "ums" I had been using: "Nope. I haven't thought as much as Napoleon, so I have *not* thought and grown poor," I said. It was a feeble attempt at humor, and you didn't laugh.

"If I hadn't read that book I'd be as poor as a church mouse. By the way, what line of work are you in?"

"Funny you should ask," I replied. "I'm a church mouse. Actually, I'm a preacher."

"Good for you, reverend. I read a book by a reverend once. Russell Conwell's *Acres of Diamonds*."

"I *have* read that one," I told him, glad that our literary paths had crossed at least once.

"He got rich too. I haven't got as much as I want, but look at me: I'm still a young man. I got time."

Your tales of being self-made were cut short because they announced our flight. It was time to board the plane. They handed us each an umbrella, and we made our way through the drizzle to the plane. The small set of stairs was supported by a couple of taut chains, and we climbed up into the cramped fuselage and took our seats. Lucky for me, our seats were right together. Once we were seated, you went on telling me how the smart man (i.e., *you*) could make a million just by getting into a positive mood about the market. I went on saying "um" at every welcome break.

Soon the little plane was sloshing down the runway and leaping with daring into the darkness. I'm not familiar with a children's story about "the little plane that could," but I thought about "the little engine that could" and wondered if the little plane could actually make it to Memphis.

Once in the air, the wind pushed us about like a feather

in a hurricane. Lightning was obvious at all times off either wing—but not very far off. Thunder was all around us. The wind and the roar of the engines kept all conversation at a minimum. I don't know what you were praying, but I was praying to live till we reached the next possible runway. I was praying for a reprieve. I'm sure that, like all the other passengers, I was confessing my sins—all the big sins and as many of the little ones as God might think significant.

I looked over at you, and all at once you clutched your chest. A grimace of agony washed across your face, and then your whole body went limp. I knew almost instinctively that you were either in heaven or hell, but wherever you were, you had left the plane and this earth forever.

On a plane as small as ours there were no flight attendants and there was no door between the cabin and the cockpit. I began shouting to the pilots. I was only a yard or two away from them, but between the headsets that covered their ears and the roar of the engines and the storm, they could not hear me. The other passengers could see what I saw, and they knew the pilots had to know.

When the sky seemed to settle for a moment, I daringly unbuckled my seat belt so I could stretch myself forward, and I whacked one of the pilots on the shoulder. He turned around just as I adroitly rebuckled my seat belt.

I pointed to you and shook your upper torso so he

could get the urgency of your condition. He grimaced in surprised understanding.

In thirty more minutes of flying, we settled below the dark ceiling of the storm. The five of us who had been delivered from the jaws of the dragon clapped weakly and sighed with relief as we landed in Memphis.

As the little plane rolled along the runway, toward the apron, I could see an ambulance waiting for you, but I knew the ambulance was just a gesture. You would trade it all too soon for a hearse. And so we parted. Me for Memphis, and you for heaven or hell.

I will never forget your bravado that night. You talked so incessantly about how well you were getting on in the world—but in this world only! You never knew at the time that you were only minutes from the only world that matters. You were like a man carrying a basket of casino chips into a world where casino chips can't be cashed in.

Jesus told the tale of a man pretty much like you. He kept building barns to store his vast wealth, and just as he completed his last storage facility, Jesus said to the people,

> "Take care! Protect yourself against the least bit of greed. Life is not defined by what you have, even when you have a lot."
> Then he told them this story: "The farm

of a certain rich man produced a terrific crop. He talked to himself: 'What can I do? My barn isn't big enough for this harvest.' Then he said, 'Here's what I'll do: I'll tear down my barns and build bigger ones. Then I'll gather in all my grain and goods, and I'll say to myself, Self, you've done well! You've got it made and can now retire. Take it easy and have the time of your life!'

"Just then, God showed up and said, 'Fool! Tonight you will die. And your barnful of goods— who gets it?'

"That's what happens when you fill your barns with Self and not with God!" (Luke 12:15–21 MSG)

I pray you are in heaven and that you went there from the tiny body of a tiny plane into the grandeur of heaven's roominess. If you're there, I wonder how important to you your gold stash really was in a place where the streets are made of it.

And if you are in heaven, I hope you have an opportunity to look earthward to study those beautiful Ivy League children of yours. If you are in heaven, look around and ask yourself in the middle of all that crystal brilliance, "Did I teach my children the virtue of the wonderful heritage that might be theirs, or did I simply school them in the futile arts of barn building and self-congratulation?"

A WRINKLE IN
ETERNITY

Solitary weeping is a form of prayer.

———— ⚘ ————

Madeleine L'Engle,
Two-Part Invention

MADELEINE
L'ENGLE

Life is the great teacher, Madeleine, and one of the lessons both Barbara and I need most is just some good, sound counsel on what to do when death comes for one of us, altering life for the both of us. I don't think I missed a single one of your books across the many years of our friendship, but the one I find myself most dependent on is *Two-Part Invention*. In its pages I am best instructed on how to face the coming separation, helping me understand that "'til death do us part" is not just a formal rite, it is a promise and a prophecy as well.

You have experienced something we have not been asked to do. Your husband, Hugh, entered heaven in September 1986, and you followed in September 2007. It is the fear of this kind of years-long separation that you and Hugh endured before you met again in heaven that so threatens my own sense of adjustment. You went through two decades of "gone-ness," and the fearsome nature of this time when he was there and you were here is what I need to pull alongside as my counsel.

You freely admitted that "the more people we love, the more vulnerable we become," yet you insisted that you "wouldn't have missed a minute of it, not any of it."[1]

You never married again. Barbara and I have talked about this situation so often. We both say we would not marry again either. I think we will stick with our guns on the matter. It's not that we think there is any sin in remarrying; it's just that we each would feel sorry for the second spouse in either of our lives. Beyond that, there is a sense of abridgement when we write so gloriously of our first love if, when it is gone, we marry again. I don't think divorced people feel that way about taking a second mate while the first one is still alive.

I had a friend who used to speak at a lot of conferences for people who had lost a spouse through divorce. Somewhere in her lectures on the subject, she would always say, "I believe in divorce because I like my second husband so much better than I liked my first."

I didn't know her first spouse, but her second was a wonderful mate, and with him she spent the rest of her life. But to consider doing that myself, I say no; I'm not in that situation, but if it happens, I see it as a resounding "No!" I don't think I could ever lay my first wife in the ground and then take a second.

Poet Robert Browning did that, and when I learned this about him, I remembered all that schmaltz in *The Barretts of Wimpole Street* about how his love was mighty enough to rescue an invalid (Elizabeth Barrett) from the clutches of an abusive father . . . even mighty enough to restore her to perfect health in the last ten years of their relationship. Then Elizabeth died, and not long after that, he married a second time.

Who was the second Mrs. Browning? Who knows? Who cares? It was the first Mrs. Browning who asked, "How do I love thee? Let me count the ways," and who wrote that delicious tribute to their love.

Madeleine, I understand your forty-year marriage of complete love; to demonstrate that love, you didn't try for a second such mate. There never was one who measured up to Hugh, I guess, and even if there was, you apparently made the decision never to force that person to live in the vise of many comparisons for however long the second marriage might last. It would not be fair—always expecting the latecomer to live up to the near sainthood of an earlier spouse.

These thoughts always remind me of the preacher who, in preaching on sin, shouted authoritatively to his congregation, "All have sinned! Nobody can live without sin!

Does anybody here know anybody who ever lived sinlessly?"

To this rhetorical question, a thin, balding man in the third row said, "Yes, I do . . . my wife's first husband."

Who would want to put a second mate through a lifetime of such comparison?

If forced to enumerate my wife's faults, I could probably name a few. Concerning myself, my wife could possibly name a few more, though I doubt if either of us would enter into such a survey. The truth is, the process of fifty years of idolizing each other's virtues has left us so in awe of each other that we always feel like Mary Poppins evaluating herself to her wards: "I'm practically perfect in every way."

I can tell, Madeleine, that you and Hugh suffered from the same protective madness. But more than that, I remember from your marriage memoir that you also had fears of the "gone-ness" feeling that comes when the first spouse dies. You confessed:

> Not long after our marriage, I wrote in my journal: "I read somewhere that one only appreciates happiness only when one is afraid of losing it. But in the world today one has to accept that fear as a kind of guest in the house and it makes the moments when it is pushed into the background more intense and more wonderful."[2]

This fear of gone-ness that stalks our happy lives for so many years before it is born as a fact is not a paper tiger; it is real. When the mourning crepe is on the door, we suddenly know that the word *two* is gone, and life is a confrontation of the simplest and most horrible of all the numbers: *ONE!* A single seat at a Broadway play. One little narrow pew place in church. The table set with one fork, one spoon, one plate, all to serve the monster called "Who's hungry?" And we are drawn to the intrigue of going to the cemetery to be near the last place we knew the presence of the one who left us. Our mate is not there, but his or her memory swims the ether of that desolation, and the gone-ness eats at us.

It is hard, this gone-ness. We rail at God; we doubt we can bear it; but somehow we do. And in the process of looking the medusa of death in the face, we find the purpose of God in the years we gave marriage and in the years when we had to give it up. That purpose is found in the story you shared of a bishop who had experienced the limit of grief and made the ultimate discovery: "I have been all the way to the bottom and it is solid."[3]

You've been in heaven for four years now, Madeleine, and what I have learned from you is that God is sufficient and there is a bottom. And this is glorious.

But also glorious is the routine of a good, godly marriage. I love what Hugh said to you repeatedly, defining the glory of your own special routine: "I love our rut."[4] The truth is, both Barbara and I can say, "We love our rut too."

I love it when we are walking in the garden—as we do every day. We also work out nearly every morning at the YMCA, and I miss this routine when it isn't in place.

Ruts have been defined as a grave with both ends kicked out. But one thing is for sure: if a routine rut is a grave, it is clearly a grave for two—a grave that ends at *the* grave. Then, past the survivor's final breath, lovers are once again together.

You ask in your book, Madeleine, "Do lovers meet again, after death?" The answer, you wrote, "is held in the mystery of the Word made Flesh," and you reminded us that faith "is not for the conceivable, but for the mysterious."[5]

Jesus said that in heaven there is neither marriage nor giving in marriage (Mark12:25), and while I cannot imagine or like the thought of not being married to Barbara, it may be the case. But the Scriptures also say that in heaven we shall know even as we are known (1 Corinthians 3:12). So if we are destined to know our mates, perhaps that eternal crown of our earthly togetherness will be extended.

I suppose many marriages fail because couples quarrel their way along a rut they despise, never having learned to find the simple glory of waking up in the morning and saying, "What a great rut is our rut." There is something of largesse in a good rut. Madeleine, you and Hugh showed us that routine togetherness is a delicious rut—perhaps the only meaningful way to enjoy the world or reckon with its pain.

During these four earth-years that you and he have been together in heaven, I trust that all the lost joy of your separation has been given back to you. I personally hope that Barbara's and my own marriage will know the elevated bliss of heaven, as I surely hope has been true for the two of you. If so, it was a good path you cleared for the rest of us.

ENTERING
HEAVEN FROM
A FARMER'S POND

Five years ago, I was enveloped by the

stillness and emptiness and loneliness

that are the companions to death. . . .

Five years ago, I put [Hope's] body in

the ground and walked away.

Today, as I remember back five years, I feel

the weight and trauma of it as if it were

yesterday. And I'm reminded how natural

death is for everyone, and yet how completely

unnatural it feels. It goes against every instinct

inside of us, and we claw to cling to life.

—— ◦୨୧୨ ——

Nancy Guthrie,
Hope

TO DICKEY

I only have one picture of you, the only picture I have of us together. I've had it now for sixty-nine years. It was taken just before you drowned.

I don't remember that day. I was only a little more than three years old, and the fog of infancy had not quite cleared from my early memory. Can I remember anything at all at that age? At times I think I do, and at times I think I don't. Yet the images that form the early mists of my being will not leave me. I'm pretty sure I saw you lying in your coffin. In fact, I know I did. It is my earliest memory of anything. I didn't cry, but I was stopped by the wonder of your closed eyes and your utter stillness. It is that image that is so unforgettable. I was not quite old enough to remember when you died, nor indeed understand what death really was.

I only know that once you were in the ground, I had the oddest sense of a vacancy in my world. There was that quiet, unspoken moment we had together, and then you were gone.

In my own childish way, I remember the quietness. The horrid stillness. And I could see that while you were there, you really were not there. The absence continued . . . and continued. I felt it. I feel it still, even though now I am old. We have unfinished business, you and I. We were here on this good earth for the blink of an eye, and yet we never spoke. We never said hello. We never said good-bye.

I wanted to write you, not to confess some way that I might have wronged you, but to tell you I have always felt this odd emptiness toward you because I think we passed like ships in the night.

If only you hadn't gone swimming. If only we could have had a real life together. But now all I hold is a photograph and an almost-memory of being held up to peer over the side of that horrid satin box.

What possessed you to go swimming that day, or what possessed you to think swimming was something you could manage? Did Mama tell you it was okay? She is gone now, as you are, and I have no one to assure me that she forbade it or concurred with your choice.

But I know this for sure: you were the fifth child and the eldest son, and I was the seventh child and third son.

Your stillness broke our family into two pieces—the four oldest girls and the four younger children. You, the center-piece of Mama's brood of nine, were gone. And I cannot tell you the times, well into adolescence, that I looked at our gallant mother and sensed that she dealt all the rest of her life with the same odd, nagging vacancy I feel that wears your name.

They say someone counseled her at the funeral, "Ethel, you should not grieve so wholeheartedly. You still have eight other children."

"I want them all," she said. "I want them all!"

They spoke of you as a kind of lost "child of promise." They obviously thought you would grow up to do honor to the family name. There were so many things I wish you could have known. And there were some things I'm glad you never had to know.

Papa and Mama divorced shortly after you died. Papa's alcoholism was finally unbearable to Mama, and she took a fearsome step for a woman with eight remaining chil-dren. All four of our older sisters married shortly after you left. Then came the war. All our eldest sisters married ser-vicemen, and our whole world was consequently plunged into a death struggle.

Izetta, our eldest sister, lost her husband in occupied Japan in 1945. We Americans won the war! And our family fortunes improved dramatically after that. But you never knew that. You took off for heaven from the muddy depths of a farm pond two years before the conflict got going.

You were ten when you got to heaven. Are you still? I've always wondered how that works. Do children there stay children forever? If not, then heaven is likely to be filled only with old people in the future. If you are still only ten years old, you'll hardly recognize me when we finally get together because I'll be in my mid-seventies at least. I'm now a very old man whom you have not seen since I was three.

I once heard an evangelist years ago preach on heaven, but not very well. He preached on it as if he didn't know anyone who had ever been there, saying in his sermon that everyone would be thirty-three years old in paradise since Jesus was thirty-three when he returned to heaven. He based his theory on 1 John 3:2: "But we know when Christ appears, we shall be like him; for we shall see him as he is" (NIV).

In the intervening years, five more members of our family have joined you in heaven, beginning with Mother. David, Patsy Ruth, and Izetta—our elder siblings—are also there now. Do you ever see them? Is heaven like that? I sometimes picture it as a great big family reunion with crocks of lemonade and iron skillets full of fried chicken.

I've heard plenty of southern gospel quartets singing about how it will be when we get there. Some have said that this life is like a mountain railway that carries us "from the cradle to the grave."[1] And then there's that old nineteenth-century spiritual that says we'll be wearing "Dem Golden Slippers" as we "walk all over God's heaven."[2]

Got your slippers yet?

I never knew you to have a pair of nice shoes. We Miller kids all went barefoot most of the year. I hope you got your slippers, though I can't remember that our barefootedness was all that important.

These are the things I think I remember. I think I remember Papa lifting me up to see you lying in your casket so I could tell you good-bye. But the sight of you lying so still choked off my words. I remember that you were wearing a little pair of overalls, I think. But our sisters tell me you were wearing a pair of brown pants and a crisply pressed and starched shirt. They were a lot older than me, so I must be mistaken. Probably I was only thinking about the way you customarily dressed.

I don't suppose it much matters how the dead are dressed, but I must confess I've never liked the notion in Revelation (3:5; 6:11; 7:9) that white robes are the dress code in heaven. Somehow, overalls just seem to suit you a little better, Dickey.

So if it's okay with the Management, and if you are to be blessed with your childhood all through eternity, it'll be okay with me if you just dress like you always did.

Let John Greenleaf Whittier's benediction be yours:

Blessings on thee, little man,
Barefoot boy with cheek of tan!

And if you can get by without the white robe, it will be a lot easier to find you.

We sure have a lot to talk about.

AN UNCOMMON MAN BENEATH A COMMON STONE

Now cracks a noble heart. Good night, sweet prince,
And flights of angels sing thee to thy rest!

———— ◇ɱɱↄ ————

William Shakespeare,
Hamlet

B ob, I cannot think of your going home to heaven without thinking of your funeral and all the odd and confused days that followed it. You were a good friend, and every good friend is a "completer person" to those who claim him or her as friend. So you were to me.

I took my natural-born virtue for leadership as far as it would go. Preaching was more my forté than leadership. I wanted to be as good at running a building program as I was at communicating from the pulpit, but I couldn't pull it off. I felt my deficiencies and knew they must have been somewhat obvious to the entire congregation.

But God was good to make us friends. When I felt the shortfall of my own leadership, you were there, helping me be all I needed to be in such a growing church. You had a five-word counsel that always fitted me with survival:

"Here's what I would do," you would say. Never bossy, never mean, never condescending, but always wise, with a touch of heaven in your intentions. When that seventeen-letter phrase filled the empty air around my confusion, I was made rich with direction. Then, and only then, I would mark the insight, tailor it, later announce it, and finally enforce it.

The completer's insight is like a big breakfast at the beginning of a long and needy day. Such needy times test one of my favorite scriptures, Romans 8:16: "The Spirit Himself bears witness that we are the children of God," and your role in my life proved the promise true. I know the Spirit's witness between us was blessed by a God who can fuse two minds into that glorious codependence that feeds the world a lavish meal. Such nurture is so much fuller than the skimpy table furnished by a single, weaker heart.

So your leave-taking enriched heaven and left earth temporarily poor. I remember and ever shall remember the ghastly day you went to heaven. The terrible accident!

You were taking some bags of yard debris to the city dump when a sudden gust of wind blew one of the bags off your truck. You stopped and got out of the cab to fetch it off the pavement and throw it back on the truck. An ordinary thing it was, but hell visited the highway that awful day. They say you saw the car coming, and the driver saw you as well. He swung the car left to avoid hitting you, and you ran to your right—precisely the wrong way to keep from being hit. In this flurry of split-second wrong decisions, you left this world.

If the mistake was yours, it was one of the few mistakes you ever made. But you were crushed into that depth of silence that never knows reprieve. Did you know that for the first few weeks after your death, I visited your grave every day? I didn't do it to be near you; I knew you weren't there. I did it because somehow being there made me remember the thousands of times I depended upon you. I did it to carry your name to God, believing the Celts were right in saying we should remember the dead in Christ to our Father in heaven, for the kingdom of God is as much in heaven as ever it is here on earth. I never went to your grave without thinking through all the advice you had given me and how your counsel lifted me to fullness.

For instance, I thought about our last building program, when I was so ill at ease about leading the church into several million dollars of debt. Your own company was in a constant state of processing big plans with immense price tags, so you spoke of all things financial with a lot more ease than I did. I was better at preaching than I was at fund-raising or funds disbursement. Somehow my own reluctance was a constant concern for you, and at every stage of building the multimillion-dollar sanctuary, you walked with me, helping me see that a limited vision would result in a limited ministry.

The further we progressed into this financial wilderness, the more you reassured me. Then, when it was time to begin the architectural phase of planning, it was you more than anyone else who helped me through. I was amazed at how you worked in your world. These plans came to be without any cost to the church. Then you did an unbelievable thing: you agreed to be not just the architectural comptroller but the general contractor and superintendent for the project.

It was here that I began to realize that you and I had become partners in the same dream. Week after week, you met with the various planning groups in the church and took each one of them very seriously. They loved working with you as you explained the legitimacy or illegitimacy of each of their ideas.

Then the project began! It was sheer poetry to watch you work, week by month for more than a year and a half, as the large, 2,400-seat sanctuary was born. My own study was a dream—beautiful beyond every description and practical beyond imagining. You felt that I deserved all the credit, and I conversely felt it was you who deserved it.

Then came that wonderful day when the building opened. It was the largest evangelical sanctuary in the city. Dignitaries—political and religious—showed up, and even more than that, there was celebratory publicity throughout Omaha. Once the project was done, our roles became somewhat separated, but our friendship remained in place. My esteem for you joined that of the whole congregation; our members knew your name as well as my own.

Then you were killed. And your death drew a pall of corporate despair over the congregation. But the weight of it settled hardest on me.

Your funeral was unquestionably the largest one I have ever preached. It was in the church you designed and built, and following the service, a long file of black cars wound its way out of the city to the small cemetery where you were laid to rest. Then, after some weeks, the gravestone arrived. It was not a large, ostentatious stone. It was a commanding, black-granite marker, older in style: a large, long sort of level obelisk. As a frequent visitor to your grave, I let the serenity of the place set my focus on heaven. I would think of you in your new estate and wonder how you got along in the rarified atmosphere of paradise.

Splendidly, I think!

It was altogether fitting that you joined the Savior whose life you so thoroughly imitated. The both of you were carpenters. Both of you were simple men with high allegiance to the truth. No wonder you were so fond of each other. You were both born to enjoy heaven and to redeem all you could of earth.

All that Saint Justin said of Jesus might be said of you:

> He grew up like any other man. He lived in a fitting way and granted each stage of development its due . . . he was known as the son of Joseph the carpenter and was without comeliness as the scriptures foretold. He was also regarded as a carpenter; for when he was among men, he made the things a carpenter makes, plows and yoke, in order to teach the symbols of justice and an active working life.[1]

This was you, Bob, never trying to hide among the ostentatious or the pretentious. You knew a greater joy . . . just being yourself. Being what God made you was the gift you gave to all of us. And it is most amazing that in being what you were, you were so much like Christ.

It never was just the two of us, was it, Bob? It was all three of us—you and me and Jesus.

GETTING DRESSED
FOR GOD

What a beautiful sight it is for God when

a Christian wrestles with pain;

when he takes up the fight against threats,

capital punishment, and torture;

when smiling he mocks at the clatter of the tools

of death and the horror of the executioner;

when he defends and upholds his liberty

in the face of kings and princes,

obeying God alone to whom he belongs;

when triumphantly and victoriously he challenges

the very one who has passed sentence upon him!

For he is the victor who has reached

the goal of his aspirations.

—— ᕬᕬ ——

The Octavius of Menicius Felix

ANNE
HERBERT

I met you the very day your incurable, inoperable carcinoma was diagnosed. You were emotionally down and so spiritually needy that you came to Christ with no pressure applied. I have always enjoyed watching new believers relish their state of grace. And for all your tears, you were 100 percent in favor of trusting God completely as you entered "the valley of the shadow."

I have walked with many "threatened saints" who were living through their last year of life. In some ways, their biographies follow a single course. There are endless trips to the clinic to monitor their state of need. There are always the same eager questions for their oncologist: How am I doing? How much time do I have left? Is there something stronger I can take to endure my pain? I read about a new cure; will it come in time to help me?

Both the fear of the future and the hope of a saving miracle intermingle in the heart. Then there is the endless regimen of pills on chair-side trays. There is also the new discovery of prayer.

It was this new calling to prayer that led me to see in you the real truth of your faith. Many cancer patients pray in one way or another, "Lord, get me out of this predicament!" Others live a life in Christ that is more celebratory; their need for God often leads them into seasons of celebration and praise. You were definitely in this camp.

The German Christian Helmut Thielicke was a pastor in Stuttgart during World War II and found himself trying to give hope to his flock crowded together in the shelters when the bombs were falling on his parish. They were American bombs, dropped by American bombers with the kind of savage firepower that Americans hoped might bring the war to a hasty conclusion.

In the terror of that place, Thielicke heard a lot of prayers. He said his people tended to pray one of two ways. Some of them prayed, "lord, save us from the BOMBS!" with *lord* in lowercase letters and *bombs* in uppercase letters. But a few prayed, "LORD, save us from the bombs!" with the emphases reversed. These latter prayers were the real prayers, he said.

May I say, Anne, that I have made the same observation about cancer patients. Some of those I have ministered to prayed, "lord, save me from this CANCER!" Others prayed, "LORD, save me from this cancer!"

You were the model. You always kept the Lord in capital letters.

I actually loved visiting you each week. You were always excited about the new things you were learning in the Psalms, and you were eager to tell me what you had only lately come to understand about the loving-kindness of the Almighty. To be sure, I watched you take your medicine quite regularly—it was like you were eating a chocolate; you seemed to actually enjoy it . . . no grimaces or frowning gulps. You wanted all the help that science could give you, never begrudging the pharmacists their assistance.

We laughed and prayed and watched the calendar. We knew there was only a year of it left for you, give or take a month or two, and every day was precious. You made no attempt to stop time, and you seemed to do your best to enjoy it. Every time you tore off a page from your calendar, you were aware it was a day you wouldn't get back. There was so much to endure, and always, a never-ending feeling that what had been lived through was the easy part. The hard part was still out there, still ahead.

Gradually the hard part came. But you made even that look easy. I remember how Maury bought you a couple of wigs and how you never missed a beat in laughing about how convenient it was to put away your hairdo at night and put it on fresh the next morning.

Sunday was your day. You never tired of hearing what I was thinking about God, and you never missed church. Your regular attendance amazed me as your pain began to increase. Maury told me that, for all your chipper pretense, you were suffering a great deal. He said on Sunday mornings you would get up very early and take a shower, and then you would be so fatigued that you would have to lie down again before getting up and putting on part of your makeup. Then you would rest again before you finished.

Finally, by church time, you were sitting in the car, ready to join us for worship. Then, after church, you had to go straight home and rest before you had the strength to change clothes for lunch. Nobody at church ever knew this part of your Sunday morning ritual.

When the dark, last days came, at last you were too weak to even sit or stand. Your pain became so acute it shut you off from your world. It is amazing how pain narrows human discourse to virtually nothing. When pain grows severe enough, the only longing we know is to be free of it. It causes us to retreat into cavernous self-absorption. When it is intense enough, we are walled away into such deep isolation we don't want to be interrupted by visits from our best friends. Even visits from our lifelong mates! There are no friends. There is no family beyond the inner wall of our screaming neurons.

It was then, dear Anne, that I didn't want to see you fight the cancer anymore. It was not that I wanted you to give in. It was, instead, an utter longing in my spirit to see you free. Maury couldn't help you; I couldn't help you either. You didn't call for me to read you any psalm, though it was the one thing you carried to the borders of your suffering. Maury was not one to sob, but I never saw his face dry the last few days you were on earth.

Then, mercifully, the angels came, and you were gone. Heaven came down and enveloped you. And suddenly you were strong and well again, as the hymn you had grown to love—Walt Harrah's "No More Night"—seemed to settle all about me in your room. I swear I almost heard the lyrics as the nurses pulled the sheet over your face and you stepped through the veil into the place where God makes all things new.

SCRUBBING UP
SAINTS

Three gates in-a de east,

Three gates in-a de west.

Three gates in-a de north,

And three gates in-a de south,

Making it twelve gates-a to de city-a, Hallelu!

Oh! What a beautiful city.

——— ◦〰◦ ———

Traditional African-American spiritual

PAUL
LITTLE

O f all the writers and influencers of evangelicalism, you were one of the most important in my life. From the time I became a pastor, I recognized that it is not possible to practice the office to which Christ called me without feeling obligated to call the world to faith. From those early days in Omaha when I was trying my best to persuade unbelievers to Christ, you were a mentor to my effort. No, not just *a* mentor, but *the* mentor.

Your books were not large, threatening volumes talking around some unimportant subject. They were insightful and incisive, and they urged me to learn the discipline of personal evangelism. I say "discipline," for the work of evangelism is arduous, and it's the most threatening part of pastoral care.

It was not easy for me, nor is it easy, I suspect, for anyone who accepts the mantle of a personal evangelist. In those days, the customary way to win people was a one-on-one effort we referred to as "confrontational" evangelism. We then moved from talking about a confrontational methodology to the friendlier modifier of "encounter"—encounter evangelism. Then, in successive decades, we left the word *encounter* and began to speak of "relational" evangelism, and finally of "lifestyle" evangelism.

Each time we weakened the adjectives, it seemed to me we weakened our whole sense of the urgency of evangelism. But in the days when I was reading your books, I felt the challenge of trying to win all to Christ that I possibly could. I reasoned that if there really was a hell to be avoided and a heaven to be gained, I needed to avoid glossing over the tough adjectives and talk to people honestly.

I think the thing you helped me to see was that some in the church were advising us to be "relevant" instead of "other-worldly" in our evangelism. What they really meant was that the pulpit should talk about getting a job, or being a sensitive father or a good citizen. These volunteer mentors said that people would rather hear about these "more practical" issues and be preached a gospel that created love and community. Why delve into the matter of eternity, so the thinking went. There were too many things about the here and now that needed to be addressed to be so other-worldly about getting people into heaven.

But while these changes in customs and approaches were swirling around us, your work with the Billy Graham organization, I think, kept you where Billy was, and that meant remaining focused on a strong proclamation of Christ and eternity.

Paul, you made a believer out of me.

Your discipline of evangelism was not a discipline that was easy to learn. The church I was attempting to plant was in suburbia, in Omaha—a very non-Bible Belt area. It was also non-Southern Baptist, which was my denomination. In fact, only one-half of 1 percent of Nebraskans were Southern Baptist; while there were 15 million Southern Baptists in America, there were virtually none in Nebraska. I knew if I was going to start a Baptist church in Omaha, I was going to have to create that congregation out of new converts to the Christian faith. It could not be done by rounding up a group of longtime Baptists who happened to be living in the area.

Since there were only ten people in the Bible study that I hoped would establish such a church, I had no reputation to defend. None of the other already-employed pastors knew I was in town. So I elected to try the Paul Little philosophy of talking to people door-to-door throughout the city.

It was a process that required more courage than I at first imagined I possessed. But I launched into a simple endeavor to talk to people who would listen in their doorways while I explained to them who I was and why I had come to town. There is nothing more fearsome, Paul, than ringing a doorbell and putting into practice a kind but effective introduction to Christ. It is a lonely feeling, really, because the witness knows that ordinary people on an ordinary day do not like to talk about God or their need for him. So the witness stands there on the stoop, ringing the bell, desperately hoping nobody's home, while those inside reluctantly answer the door, wishing the "God-man" was at somebody else's door.

I would never have started doing this at all had I not realized the most important issue in every life is the need for Christ to be centered in that soul. But in spite of the adverse sociology that evangelism represents, there is a sense of earnestness about it. And almost every conversion I was involved with was born in this dialogue.

That door-to-door work had a rather immediate payoff in my way of viewing things: the church averaged two additions every week for twenty-five years. The little ten-member congregation with which I began the church became a formidable fellowship of three thousand members because I stood up to my screen-door phobias in the practice of leading men and women to Christ. More than you knew, Paul, you inspired my whole notion of church growth.

But now that I've been honest about all you inspired in my life, I would like to wrangle through the open way in which God works "his wonders to perform."[1] In the early summer of 1975, you were killed in a tragic accident. All of us who loved you and knew you—even if you didn't know us—were heartbroken at our loss. I could not imagine any good coming out of such a tragedy. But my coming of age as a writer was intricately bound up in your heavenly homegoing.

I was completely unknown at the time, and I had just published a book called *The Singer*. By the oddest turn of events, you had been scheduled to introduce your new book at the Christian Booksellers Association that year. Your death prevented you from honoring that appointment, so someone on the program committee, who happened to have read my new book, called and asked me to take your place at a luncheon where you had been asked to speak. I felt totally unworthy to be your replacement, but I agreed to do it.

Paul, to be a stand-in for you was most humbling. When I actually got to the convention center, I faced multiple moments of self-examination. When I checked into the hotel, my room was still registered under your name. The program folder at the luncheon still listed you as the speaker. Even the little place card where I sat had your printed name marked through and my own name entered in pencil. Each time I encountered one of these moments, it reminded me that I was not you, their first choice.

But if there is any virtue in confronting repeated humblings, it must first be a good dose of anti-egotism. There's no harm in being reminded that no one is really anything apart from the plan of God.

Being the pastor of a fledgling church in Nebraska, this was the largest crowd I had ever spoken to. Further, I was the speaker at the third of three luncheons for the week. At the first luncheon, Johnny Cash, who had just published *Man in Black*, was the honoree. At the second, Catherine Marshall, who had just published *Something More*, was being honored. At the third luncheon, you were to be the guest of honor, but you were in heaven and I was the earthbound novice summoned to take your place. My discomfort was heightened by my publisher, who patted me unenthusiastically on the back as I was about to walk to the microphone and said, "You'd better be good!"

I've never forgotten his saying that, and I've never really forgiven him.

I walked to the microphone and, without personalizing the occasion, began an eighteen-minute monologue on *The Singer*, a fairly poetic metaphor on the life of Christ. It has a rather emotional ending, and when it was over, a kind of quiet occupied the mood of the audience. It was so quiet that I was uncomfortable with the silence. I walked back to my seat and sat down before there was even a stir.

Then someone in the far corner of the room began to applaud. Others joined in, and finally the applause was thunderous throughout the auditorium. Then they were all on their feet in an extended ovation that lifted my spirits immensely. At last I felt free to be a tad arrogant when my publisher said, "Neither Johnny nor Catherine got standing ovations, but you did." He seemed proud to walk out of the banquet hall with me.

I signed several hundred books after that luncheon, all for people in the bookseller world, and the book literally took off in national sales. I also took off as a writer. Immediately after that luncheon, I was so elated I could have flown home without the airplane. Nevertheless, I condescended and checked in at the American Airlines ticket counter for the return flight.

Paul, I'm guessing that heaven is much greater than that Anaheim convention. But if you had not gone to heaven, I wonder if I ever would have become a best-selling author. I doubt it. I owe you so much for teaching me all about personal evangelism and church growth. But I also owe you far more.

In some ways, your homegoing made my own "on-going" possible. Truly, the Lord "moves in mysterious ways, his wonders to perform."[2] I am not sorry you went to heaven, for I read it is a glorious place. And yet I am mystified at how our fortunes were more entangled than we knew. I have a feeling that when we finally do meet in heaven, we will realize that God wastes no sorrows and uses the worst tragedies in miraculous ways.

We never met, but my fortune has always been so bound up with yours that I know we shall. That will be a great day in the land where Christ is the mortar of all friendship.

THE TRUTHS THAT DEAD MEN SPEAK

In Reading gaol by Reading town
There is a pit of shame,
And in it lies a wretched man
Eaten by teeth of flame,
And in a burning winding sheet he lies,
And his grave has got no name.

And there, till Christ call forth the dead,
In silence let him lie:
No need to waste the foolish tear,
Or heave the windy sigh:
The man had killed the thing he loved,
And so he had to die.

—— ⬥⬥⬥ ——

Oscar Wilde,
The Ballad of Reading Gaol

You died thirty-odd years before I was ever born, but your words remain for me one of the single greatest truths that dead men speak, and for the last many decades of my own life, I have turned to you again and again. It is always to the same poem that I turn. Beyond the Bard and his classic insights or even Saint Paul with his elegant Christology, I find you third in line to claim earthly influence over me. Your words! They ring like a warning bell behind my every decision—before my every thought-out action.

While you sojourned there, imprisoned in Reading Gaol, the crush of your aloneness left you a disconsolate automaton. Your vast popularity as a playwright . . . gone. Your family, in the press of your trial and sentence, abandoned you. Your beautiful sons were made to avoid you. You were the butt of jokes by your countrymen. Your literary works were formidable, but there was no fan mail. Just a condemnation to live within the dripping walls and see only a "tent of sky." And in this dismal place, you contemplated all that had brought you there.

The only reading material you had was left lying about to encourage you toward repentance.

> For the Doctor said that Death was but a
>   scientific fact:
> And twice a day the Chaplain called and left
>   a little tract.

The purposelessness of shuffling along the iron-barred walls—plodding through the intestines of Reading Gaol— was the purgatory that made you weep your repentance. And "while the hangman with his little bag went shuffling through the gloom," you trembled as you groped your way into your "numbered tomb."

Then "the cock crew, the red cock crew, but never came the day."

The prison killed you, I think. Oh, you lived a score of months once you were released, but you died in Reading Gaol, I'm pretty sure. Still, your painful incarceration became for you a bully pulpit, and your sermon was elegance to all who saw it and treasured it. You made voyeurs of us all, for you let us see that pitiful inmate of yours.

He was on death row when you met him. Reading was the death of both of you. But only he left there with his death certificate in hand. The prison took your life gradually, but it took his in a few seconds of pain at the place of scaffolds and rope.

It was only fair: the man had murdered the woman he loved in an act of rage. He caught her at her infidelity, and he murdered both her and her illicit lover in their faithless bed. But his hopelessness was meat that both of you had to eat, because right or wrong, he faced the gallows, and there he died.

> He looked upon the garish day
> With such a wistful eye;
> The man had killed the thing he loved,
> And so he had to die.

But the man on death row is not to be singled out. You testified, Oscar, that all men kill the thing they love. That's why you were in Reading Gaol, wasn't it? You were the Shakespeare of the Victorian era. You were a master at writing your plays and novels and poems. You were the toast of English society. You had a lovely home, princely sons. These were all God's gifts to you.

But when the judge rapped his gavel and sentenced you to prison for sodomy, shame rolled over you. Hot burning shame! Your wife turned her face away. It was you who died every day for two years because

> . . . he does not win who plays with Sin
> In the secret House of Shame.

The executed wife-murderer was taken from the scaffold and thrown in a pit of lime with no requiem. The lime turned his chalky bones to ash. The lime pit in your odd metaphor of shame served the same purpose for you:

> This too I know—and wise it were
> If each could know the same—
> That every prison that men build,
> Is built with bricks of shame.

The legacy you left has had a powerful effect on me, and the warning of your words from jail have helped me see that all men, or at least many men, do indeed kill the thing they love. They make their own prison, which raises bars and walls against all God called them to be. When I watch other pastors trade their entire lives for a moment of sin, I think of your words. I realize that every human being I know is in danger of killing his or her future and throwing dreams into the lime pits of shame.

Most do it simply. A preacher I much admired spent

his first forty years of ministry building a church, and his last ten years killing it. In his case, he couldn't let go. He held on long after old age had made him an anemic replica of the handsome young visionary who had started the church. By hanging on too long, he unwittingly killed the thing he loved.

I knew a pastor who in a moment of weakness had an illicit affair. He was in middle age before he sinned, and the shame of his unguarded moments rose up against him. His congregation of many years had no choice but to fire him. His wife wept for their lost reputation. He bowed his head in shame before his sons, to whom he had once taught the godly lessons of propriety that he himself could not honor.

What was there to do then but to enter his own Reading Gaol? He died in shame because he forgot the poet's warning and remembered too late that men do kill the thing they love.

I am seventy-five now, Oscar. And yet I want you to know that I never take a day for granted. I guard myself against the kind of condemnation that took from you your sterling life of reputation and literary genius. You were good at your art . . . really good. Naturally, you got it all back. And those of us who admire your work will treasure the wonderful way you, an Irish playwright, gave the world all that you gave it.

For you, the end was costly. Fortunately your writings, years later, brought you to the honest place in history no one could keep you from owning.

Again and again you have lured me back to Reading Gaol. I return to hear you cry again that we who do exalt the work we love do not misspend our lives. But shame itself is redeeming, and for that I am always grateful. For when the world rejects us, we turn of necessity to Christ. It was true for you too.

For all its horror, Reading Gaol held for you the presence of the Savior who walked your same stone-and-steel hallways. There he came, bless him—the Christ. No stranger to prisons, he! He lifted you with wounded hands and found you all over again. Your brokenness became, for you, a door to grace.

These are the happy words: even those who kill the thing they love are candidates for grace. And these may be the happiest words you ever wrote—and the truest:

> Ah! Happy they whose hearts can break
> And peace of pardon win!
> How else may man make straight his plan
> And cleanse his soul from sin?
> How else but through a broken heart
> May Lord Christ enter in?

THE LOOK OF
COMMON MARTYRS

Much of the Muslim world is a parched land.

. . . Rocky promontories push their way upward

into the harsh glare of the desert sun. . . . The

religion, Islam, . . . shares many of these same

characteristics. To the traveler in the region, the

predominance of a harsh, hard, and stubborn

terrain presses itself on the mind, making it

impossible to ignore the analogy to a religious life

that is equally harsh, hard, and stubborn.

. . . It is hard to imagine what it would mean to

be a woman in this place, . . . but here it is a man's

world . . . those few women who brave the streets

scurry along with tentative and apologetic steps.

—— ◦∽∽∽つ ——

Calvin Miller and Dan Crawford,
Walking the Walk

I have only known a few martyrs in my life, and when I knew them, they seemed so utterly warm and congenial that I would have found it impossible to imagine that anyone anywhere could ever hate them. They were basically world lovers who would not hurt a flea. They served their Lord by going into the most desperate of worlds to do what they could to turn the enemies of God into his best friends.

So it was with you, Martha. I never met anyone with a freer laugh than you. I never met anyone who found Christ more essential to the nitty-gritty than you. You truly existed to call the world to be its best self.

I regret not taking time with you. In all honesty, I was intrigued at your commitment, but you were involved in the high calling of medicine in a world of filth and typhus and poverty, and I would have hated myself if I had diverted you from that crush of human need to which you had dedicated your life.

Throughout my brief time in Yemen, I never met an Arab citizen I suspected of liking me. I would have liked to be considered a friend, but I was too Christian, too white, too American. The only place in all the world where I have ever had people throw rocks at me was in Yemen. They were pretty big rocks too.

I was doing nothing to abet their anger. I was simply walking down the street with a group of fellow missionaries when the stones started flying. When I have shared this story with others, they often ask, "What did you do? When the rocks started flying, what did you do?"

I always tell them, "I just prayed they would hit the other missionaries."

In truth, there was little that was humorous at the time. Later on the day of my "stoning," I met with you and some other missionaries on a flat rooftop for a Scripture-and-prayer session. It was always necessary to have someone posted as lookout for the police because all Christian gatherings are illegal.

I wondered that day how each of the great Christian doctors who served with you could give so much to people who seemed to appreciate it so little. In some ways it seems to the rest of us that Christian missionaries are naïve. It's as though they live a charmed life and pay little attention to the world as it really is. I count it all joy to have prayed with you and talked with you and read the Scriptures with you. The coffee was great, and I drank it feeling as though I was having an audience with the queen.

The day after we prayed, I saw you in your Ford Bronco. The car was full of women—everyone in a burka. Their only view was through that long slit in the headdress. Yours was the only face I could see. It was a surreal moment for me.

I asked a Yemeni friend if this was a customary outing for you. He told me that *burka* should be Arabic for "maternity dress" because so many Arab men sire children, and the long, flowing burkas hide their wives' pregnancy from the public. He further told me that you, Martha, would deliver their babies for only four dollars apiece—or less if the women didn't have it.

He said you were a real hit for two reasons. The Arab women didn't feel comfortable having a man examine them, and the Arab men didn't like the idea of white male doctors examining or even seeing their wives. So, he said, much of the obstetric work at the clinic fell to you. He said you ran a shuttle to get these women to and from the clinic.

Everything I heard about you added to the esteem I had already given you. I have always believed that humanity is the porch of divinity, and in this you exceeded even that fictitious woman who appears in Proverbs 31. Remember her?

> She is worth far more than rubies.
> Her husband has full confidence in her. . . .
> She selects wool and flax and works with
>   eager hands.
> She is like the merchant ships, bringing her
>   food from afar. . . .
> She considers a field and buys it. . . .
> When it snows, she has no fear for her
>   household; for all of them are clothed.
> (vv. 10–11, 13–14, 16, 21 NIV)

Poor thing, she couldn't drive a Bronco and deliver a thousand, four-dollar babies. But you did, Martha, and not just that: every one of those women you helped was a candidate to be the friend of Jesus. Still, conversion comes hard in Yemen. Anyone who converts loses employment, family, and their place in the community. Sharia Law is severe, including amputations, stonings, and decapitations. It is an especially hard world for women—a world you seemed to conquer with more Christian grace than anyone I've ever known.

And always, your warm humanity dominated your severe desert existence. You dropped a huge grenade of gentility in the hard Arabian Desert. Shortly before I met you, you had been kidnapped by some Yemeni car thieves who tried to steal your Bronco. But you prayed for them, and the new car they hoped to steal suddenly malfunctioned. It wouldn't start. And its refusal to start drew a large number of bystanders. Finally the would-be thieves fled the scene, and when someone asked you what caused them to let you go and take off for the hills, you said they just took one good look at you and decided they would rather have your car. Perhaps, because of your prayer life, they got neither one.

Once they were apprehended and thrown in prison, you often stopped by to see them and to do your best to win them to Christ. You were never able to accomplish that pair of conversions, but in an odd turn of justice, your abductors were hanged by the government. It is hard to understand that those who can commit such horrendous acts of savagery and terrorism still seem to have a high respect for women—even American women. And in the will of God, you soon got your car back, filled it up with pregnant women darkly dressed, and went on with your four-dollar baby ministry.

Just before you were killed, you dropped me a letter in which you said of those you were trying to bring to the Savior:

They have lied about us to the police, the courts, the patients and their families, stolen personal and hospital goods, eaten in my home and then come back to rob it. . . .

Living here has made many things in the Bible real. Jesus came into a hostile environment. . . . It must have hurt when he came unto his own and they received him not. . . . Every day there were people trying to catch him in his words, to cause him problems with the government by twisting his truth into lies.[1]

Jesus said we were to pray for our enemies and those who despitefully use us. You practiced the art of loving your enemies. It is probably true of every martyr that they practice daily the art of giving their lives away so that when it is time to give them up, they have settled the issue of Galatians 2:20. How many times did you read that passage?

I am crucified with Christ: nevertheless, I live; yet not I, but Christ liveth in me: and the life which I now live in the flesh I live by the faith of the Son of God, who loved me, and gave himself for me.

It was doubtless on such a day that a gunman entered your clinic and fired the horrible succession of bullets that delivered you to the realm where you could meet the Christ your soul adored. And how did you find heaven, Martha? It was not the gaudy harem room of the Muslim terrorist-martyrs who killed their way to the honor of Allah. No, it was a higher heaven than that, wasn't it?

In the meantime, you lived out the doctrine of F. B. Meyer, who said, "The tears of life belong to its interlude and not its finale."

They say ten thousand Muslims attended your funeral. If so, you might well claim to have made Jesus more obvious than you knew. The finale swung the gates, and ten thousand people who may never confess Christ saw, for one moment, that a fearless woman who never made anyone afraid had conquered all those who feed on fear.

Your passing may have been fraught with momentary terror, but a repeating rifle is such a temporary thing. And all your wounds were sutured in the presence of One who earned his own scars in the same unfeeling world where you got yours, and in much the same way.

DINNER IN ANAHEIM

I realize that in one important

sense I haven't lost him.

—— ᏬᏴᎥ᎐ ——

Luci Shaw, referring to the death

of her husband, Harold Shaw

All that was ever ours is ours forever.

—— ᏬᏴᎥ᎐ ——

Elisabeth Elliot

HAROLD
SHAW

I only met you once, but it was at a pivotal point in my life's calling. You won't remember it. I was thirty-nine years old at the time and pastor of a very small church in Omaha. In the months that preceded our meeting, I had suffered as any young seminarian might. I was trying to plant a church with very little money and almost no denominational help. In the inner, spiritual turmoil of those days, I spent a lot of time writing in my journal—and sometimes just writing on the walls of my unanswering mind.

One of the pieces that emerged from my disconsolation was my book titled *The Singer*. It had a rather eager effect on Christian people who, like me, were not winning the war against their own worst self-perceptions. But all of a sudden I was "successful," having been invited to speak at the annual international booksellers convention.

Of course, I didn't know anyone there. In fact, I hardly knew myself! But Luci—your dear wife and my only important poetic fan in the beginning—was taken with my book, and through her social engineering I got invited to have dinner with the two of you. No one who knows Luci could ever claim not to be enchanted with her. She is warm and alive with a kind of blithe spirit that charms the world. And I was taken with her spirit and her ability to make me feel important. Hers is a gift, always functioning to defeat the gravity of dull, uninformed conversation.

But it was you who on that occasion drew me up to the next level of self-worth. It was you, Harold! For unlike Luci and even myself, who were artists, you were what I once would have considered a cold-hearted businessman. Only you weren't cold-hearted; you were warm and certain. You saw with a clear eye, and you thanked me for being a writer and for agreeing to have dinner with you. It was an odd gratitude, seeing that no one else had even asked to have dinner with me. But I said, "You're welcome!" just to keep from seeming ungrateful.

Then the rest of the evening was given to prophecy, and you were the prophet! *The Singer* was but the first of all I should publish, you said. *Brilliant* would never have been your adjective, nor *genius* your noun. But the best prophecies are atmospheric. They are not spoken. They fly from the soul of the prophet and hang in the air. Like fireflies on a humid night, they flash, then they lie as dark warmth where no eye sees them. Yet every perceptive heart knows they are still alive, gathering that divine amperage to flash again and again throughout life.

At that time in your own life, Harold, *The Living Bible* was Tyndale's pursuit. And everyone knew you were the locomotive who brought that publishing event into the twentieth century. What a gift! You were the man, Harold, and yet you were unspoiled by any hint of egotism. You did what needed to be done so that a weary King James culture could find God's Word more accessible. Yours was a noble dream, a real achievement.

That night when you treated me to a sensational evening was, for this one dreamer, a real reward, and I thank you. It wasn't just your prophecies of hope that gave me all I came to cherish. You provided for me a snapshot of what a great marriage would look like. I suddenly saw in you and Luci a single icon of commitment. Forgive me if I read values into your marriage that weren't there, but I could see in you that left-brained architect of a solid planet around which Luci's poetic soul could freely orbit. Yours was the gift of gravity that gave her the artistic freedom to track the world in circles without being totally lost in bilious orbits.

I could see, it seems to me, that Luci loved and admired you for keeping her world in place. In a far lesser way, I could see you, Harold, in my own dear wife, whose attention to concrete existence has been an anchor to my own soul. How much you are alike. And how good it is to see such half-souls put together in such whole ways.

In the anonymous work *The Cloud of the Unknowing*, the writer examines the thumb-worn story of Mary and Martha all over again. Before I read the work, I, like most, always saw the ever-busy Martha as the culprit of Jesus' parable. Who could ever admire *her*? Martha, that left-brained automaton! Recipe-clipper! Budgetary efficiency expert! Non-poetic drudge!

Mary, on the other hand, I saw as the devoted, spiritual, deep, thoughtfully artistic soul—half-piety, half-poetry.

Then I read *The Cloud of the Unknowing*, and suddenly I saw the truth: they were both good women.

Jesus said Mary had chosen the better part. But the author of *The Cloud of the Unknowing* was trying to say that the world is only complete when there are enough people interested in facts to bake good prosaic bread so that those who are only interested in poetry can do the eating. When the kingdom operates that way, the fortress is whole. And when marriages operate that way, families are whole.

Two hours in a hotel restaurant in Anaheim taught me this, and you were the teacher, Harold. I wish I had told you this back then. But since I didn't, I am counting on this letter to heaven to get it through to you now. These were gifts I think you never knew you gave, but it is high time you did. Shakespeare's Lear said on one occasion, "How sharper than a serpent's tooth to have a thankless child!"[1] He also said in *Two Gentlemen of Verona*, "He does not love who does not show his love!"[2]

In this note to you, I want to repent of my own thanklessness for these lessons I never acknowledged. I may be wrong about much of this, but this is how I see it. And I know from Luci's book *God in the Dark* that she too saw you in this very concrete way I observed on that long-ago night in 1975.

When you left her for the real world of heaven, she lamented your absence in a book I have treasured a long time. I own almost all of Luci's books, but this is my favorite. I don't know if much reading takes place in heaven, but I somehow know that even in heaven, you must also have read this and cherished the relationship that was interrupted in your homegoing. A week and a half after your memorial service, Luci wrote about a dead oak tree in the yard of your home that was cut down by some friends.

She watched as the men brought down the massive tree, and she wrote:

> It's painful to witness the fall of such a giant, to
> see it treated with such indignity after all those

solid years of growth, just as it's hard to see a good man shrivel into a helpless shell . . . and disposed of.[3]

A week later the men returned and cleaned up the tree's remains, hauling away the last pieces of wood and digging the ashes out of the cavity where the stump had been burned. Soon, Luci wrote,

> you would hardly know that a tree had been there, though its invisible shape . . . still remains in my mind, and its roots still exist in some subterranean place—like Harold, whose unseen force still pervades my life and thinking, even though his visible presence is gone.[4]

The visible presence, Harold, was the reality with which you crowned every moment. Luci lived with it and knew its security and promise. I only touched it for one evening many years ago, but it clothed my unfinished neediness with a sense of why I was in the world. That, I think, is the greatest gift one can give to another.

THE MADONNA AND THE CHILD-MAN

Arise sweet child, never destined to become a man,

You're soon to die, exactly as you came.

A small, illiterate, dependent soul,

Who never learned your mother's name.

She never did resent your failure to mature,

She accepted you exactly as you came,

And never could have loved you more,

Had you the wherewithal to call her name.

Die now, at the mystic edge of manhood.

Enter heaven with no earthly blame

And wait there quietly until she comes,

Then welcome her by calling out her name.

—— ०ಾಾಿ ——

C. M.,
Journal entry

BUBBA
AND
NOLA

I wish I could have seen your glorious reunion, Bubba and Nola. I wish I could have seen your face, Nola, when you arrived in heaven and Bubba called you Mother for the first time. You had been waiting all your life to hear him say it, hadn't you? And Bubba, surely you knew—after your first moment in heaven—that you had been waiting all your life to say it.

I will never forget that moment in Bubba's fifteenth year when I watched you, Nola, feeding your son his cereal and then dutifully wiping his chin after every spoonful. I commented on how you were a true Madonna with child.

You decried the Madonna label and lamented that Bubba, throughout his life, had never been able to call you by your name. There were no tears when you said it. Most of the crying had come earlier in your life. You had cried fifteen years earlier when the doctor told you that Bubba's cerebral palsy was so advanced he would never have the motor skills to live on his own. You cried even more when the doctor told you your son would have to sit tied in a chair, unable to remain upright on his own. He would never be able to control his own bowel movements nor hold his own cup or spoon. Worst of all, he was not educable; he would never outgrow his condition.

Those were the days when you cried, sometimes uncontrollably. You operated out of loving duty. God had given you Bubba, and you knew it was because he trusted you with the important task of loving and caring for him.

Nola, you were owned from the very first by a strong code of dietary discipline, well aware that if you gave Bubba the candy and desserts that light up every child's eyes, he would soon grow too large for you to care for. Unfortunately, Bubba, the sweets that would have delighted you also would have left you unmanageable. So your mom knew she had to study nutrition and feed you well but never overfeed you.

Bubba, you weighed a comfortable thirty-two pounds. This weight made you healthy and strong for the twenty years your mother lifted you from bed to chair to high-chair to wheelchair. This weight made you easier to bathe. And how you loved the bathtub, Bubba. It might as well have been an Olympic-sized swimming pool.

Unfortunately for your mom, even in the tub, you had to be held up out of the water. Six inches of bathwater was enough to destroy you without her necessary keeping.

You read the Bible to your son, Nola, and often. I always wondered about this. As far as Bubba knew, it might as well have been the *Analects of Confucius* or the *Bhagavad Gita*. But the longer I knew of your habit, it was increasingly clear to me that the daily readings were a tryst for three: the two of you and God.

It was your opinion, Nola, that God's Word read aloud held a power all its own. One of your favorite scriptures was from Isaiah 55:9–11 (NIV):

As the heavens are higher than the earth,
  so are my ways higher than your ways
  and my thoughts than your thoughts.
As the rain and the snow come down from heaven,
  and do not return to it without watering the earth
  and making it bud and flourish,
  so that it yields seed for the sower
  and bread for the eater,
  so is my word that goes out from my mouth:
  it will not return to me empty,
  but will accomplish what I desire
  and achieve the purpose for which I sent it.

It was odd, Bubba, how you seemed to listen . . . nay, not "seemed to" but actually *did* listen. And the warmth of a Madonna and her child-man caused me to see the Bible in a new way.

God has a way with his Word that passes the senses and stops in the heart. I could see that happening for you, Bubba. It wasn't that your ear transmitted the reading to your brain. It was that your whole being was sponging up the moment and transferring the gold of God directly to your bank account in heaven. Seeing you absorb the good news, I knew for the first time that heaven transcends ordinary physiology and stores intention alone in a distant, waiting place beyond the moment, beyond the stars.

So how was it when you finally broke all your earthly tethers, Nola? You didn't at first recognize your son, did you? That's the point of transcendence. Once we are content to give up this fragile and sickly flesh, we are clothed with such a powerful radiance that we no longer know our old forms. We are like Mary Magdalene who, upon seeing Jesus after he came back from the grave, thought him to be the gardener (John 20:15).

I know what you thought, Nola, on seeing Bubba after your long separation. You thought, *What a polished and handsome young man.* Maybe you even talked to him awhile, marveling at his wit and charm. Then, like Mary Magdalene, you got it. This was Bubba! *Your* Bubba, who sat unbound and yet upright in his chair. It was from his handsome chin that you once wiped the gruel. This was really him, who loved splashing in the bathtub while you tended to his every need. This was your son, with a new address at the corner of Platinum and Gold in the most beautiful city you could ever imagine. And you could see it all.

You may have remembered then how you once read to Bubba divine words that floated in the air all around him. You once merely counted on Revelation 21:1–5 to be true. Now you owned those words and that world:

> Then I saw a new heaven and a new earth, for the first heaven and the first earth had passed away. (v. 1 NIV)
>
> *Who cares about that earth, anyway? It was full of weeping mothers and sickly children.*

> And I saw the Holy City, the new Jerusalem, coming down out of heaven from God. (v. 2 NIV)
>
> *You always knew it was there, didn't you, Nola? You could stand the corrupt hopelessness of Omaha because you always knew the new Jerusalem was in the process of coming down and its descent was your assent.*

> And I heard a loud voice from the throne saying,

"Look! God's dwelling place is now among the people, and he will dwell with them. They will be his people, and God himself will be with them and be their God." (v. 3 NIV)

In short, wherever God is, is heaven. Streets of gold and gates of pearl do not make a heaven. Only the indwelling presence that transforms cerebral palsitics into paragons of health and intelligence makes heaven, heaven.

"He will wipe every tear from their eyes. There will be no more death or mourning or crying or pain, for the old order of things has passed away." (v. 4 NIV)

Good riddance, old order. Hello, splendor! Make room for Nola and Bubba.

He who was seated on the throne said, "I am making everything new!" (v. 5 NIV)

Hello, heaven!

I can just imagine how it all went, Nola, when you first saw your son in heaven. No doubt you grabbed him in a grand embrace and said, "Bubba! Bubba, it's really you!" And of course, Bubba said, "It's me, all right, but if you don't mind, Mother, people up here call me John."

THERE'S
A MAN
GOING 'ROUND
TAKING NAMES
. . . IN INK!

And I heard a voice in the midst

of the four beasts. . . .

And I looked, and behold a pale horse:

And his name that sat on him was Death,

And Hell followed with him.

—— ✺ ——

Revelation 6:6, 8 (KJV)

We never met, but like a million other souls I was fascinated by your music. You went to heaven only a year after you released one of the most captivating bits of surrealism ever penned. I have long been fascinated that your folksy apocalypse, "When the Man Comes Around," should ever have become such a rich and final bit of balladeering.

The song opens with a quote from Revelation 6:1:

> And I heard, as it were the voice of thunder, one
> of the four beasts saying, Come and see. And I
> saw, and behold a white horse.

And then you allege the quaint cry of judgment on the human race with a quote from the long-dead folk icon

Lead Belly (Huddie William Ledbetter): "There's a man going 'round takin' names."

This Ledbetter apocalyptic hero is the great decider of "who is free and who's to blame," constantly acknowledging that in the judgment we won't all be "treated the same."

I am willing to abandon my all-consuming interest in this recording of yours, Mr. Cash, if you could just tell me why this song, with lyrics that are almost totally someone else's—either Lead Belly's or Saint John's—seemed to grip your soul so firmly during your last few months of life. I have listened to it over and over. There are fifteen biblical phrases lifted directly from the Bible—many, though not all, taken directly from the book of Revelation. Other references to Jesus' coming are taken directly from the little Apocalypse of Saint Matthew: the story of bridesmaids trimming their lamps for the second coming of Jesus, the Son of Man.

Lead Belly was ever in and out of prison, thus sharing a strangely touching similarity to your own focus on Fulsom. But the timing, Mr. Cash, the timing! You released the song in 2002 and died in 2003. And I have heard that old men constantly count the time left to them in a grown-up, furious interest in the Second Coming. John—himself an old man—received his apocalypse, it would seem, when his own life was all but gone. "Voices callin', voices cryin'" and the cycle of life leads you to conclude what is ever true and sometimes, it would seem, pointless—for "some are always being born and some are always dyin'!"

I never award anyone heaven nor condemn anyone to hell, but I believe you had a good grip on eternity because you affirm what I've always believed: that wise men bow down and cast their crowns "when the man comes around."

So it was that in 2003 he came around for you.

An old man you were by that time! And it would seem that, like another old man—John the apostle—you too saw heaven open and saw the pale horse of death. And like John, who saw the Son of Man, you also saw the Man come around—and takin' names he was. Presumably he wrote "Johnny Cash" into the ledger, that proverbial Book of Life in Revelation 20:11–12, 15 (NIV):

> Then I saw a great white throne and him who was seated on it. The earth and the heavens fled from his presence, and there was no place for them. And I saw the dead, great and small, standing before the throne, and books were opened. Another book was opened, which is the book of life. The dead were judged according to what they had done as recorded in the books. . . . Anyone whose name was not found written in the book of life was thrown into the lake of fire.

It was your final epitaph, Mr. Cash. And what I like about it is that, for all your severity, something in both you and the apostle reported the scenario without necessarily agreeing to it. Both of you seemed to see so clearly that there is a judgment where all will not be treated the same.

In this final judgement there are the general books of all the dead, great ledgers of all humanity. And there is also one smaller book, *the* book, called the Book of Life. In it is the list of all those who have called Christ "Lord." The other books are records of universal transgressions. The deeds of the righteous and the wicked must be distinguished: after all, Hitler and Clara Barton deserve vastly different treatment in the next life because of how they behaved and what they believed in this one.

There has to be a hell, I suppose, or there is not much of a moral point to heaven.

There is in Scripture a God of love. More than that, says 1 John 4:8, God *is* love. We do not have a God who enjoys throwing people into hell. For anyone who insists on going there, the God called Love weeps, and as he weeps—as Lead Belly and the apostle and you, Mr. Cash, can clearly see—he has a Son, the Man who goes around taking names. And those names are clearly recorded in the Book of Life.

I am roughly the same age as you were, Mr. Cash, when you saw the pale horse. I too have joined the council of old ones who have visited the old man's Revelation first recorded on the Isle of Patmos. At times I fancy the truth. At times I treasure the truth.

There's a man going 'round taking names. I want to be sure he's got mine.

I actually caught sight of the Man. I met him in the coronary ward at St. Vincent's Hospital a year ago. I had a heart attack. I was one of the two-thirds who survive their first one, and I am grateful. But I'm pretty sure I saw that man takin' names, and I could see, just over the corner of his ledger, my name was there.

As you alleged, Mr. Cash, "The whirlwind is in the thorn trees." I can't exactly unravel the metaphor except to say, with Paul, that we must "[redeem] the time, because the days are evil" (Ephesians 5:15–16 KJV). I don't know how your seventy-odd years seemed to go by, but mine have been but a wisp of smoke in a strong wind (James 4:14). I have not yet seen the pale horse of death, but I have heard him stomping his steel hooves, restless in his stable.

And if I listen when it's quiet, hushed and midnight,
I can hear the stable doors creaking open,
And I sense it, as surely as I am three score and fifteen
    years . . .
I hear it and I know it—the pale horse snorts and stomps
    and rears against the gates.

I am a shy equestrian, newly released form the coronary
    ward,
Yet I am not afraid.
I have waited all my life for this ride.
When the man comes around,
It will be for me, even as D. L. Moody is reported to have
    said on his deathbed:
"Earth is receding,
 Heaven is descending."
This is my coronation day!

—*C. M., 2011*
Birmingham, Alabama

Notes

Meeting Mama's God: *Ethel Miller*

1. Calvin Miller, *A Covenant for All Seasons* (Wheaton, IL: Shaw, 1995), 18.

To a Man Whose God Was on the Gridiron: *Ed Pattison*

1. Calvin Miller, *The Singer* (Downer's Grove, IL: InterVarsity, 1975), 129.

The Roar of Impact, The Hush of Heaven: *Todd Beamer*

1. Lisa Beamer, *Let's Roll* (Carol Stream, IL: Tyndale, 2002), 250–51.
2. Ibid., 232–33.
3. Ibid.

The Man Who Celebrated Corpuscles: *Paul Brand*

1. Paul Brand and Philip Yancey, *In His Image* (Grand Rapids, MI: Zondervan, 1984), 43.
2. Miller, *A Covenant for All Seasons*, 2–4.
3. Brand and Yancey, *In His Image*, 57–58.

Narnia on the Way: *George Sayer*

1. Isaac Watts, "Hill of Zion," 1868.
2. Albert Brumley, "I'll Fly Away," written 1929, published 1932.
3. James M. Black, "When the Roll Is Called Up Yonder," 1893.
4. Edgar Page Stites, "Beulah Land," 1875–76.
5. Sanford F. Bennett, "In the Sweet By and By," 1868.
6. Carrie E. Breck, "Face to Face with Christ, My Savior," 1898.

A Grief Observed: *C. S. Lewis*

1. C. S. Lewis, *The Last Battle* (New York: Macmillan, 1952), 172.
2. Ibid., 9.
3. Ibid.
4. Ibid., 19.
5. Ibid., 52.
6. Ibid., 32.
7. Ibid., 59.
8. C. S. Lewis, *The Great Divorce* (New York: Macmillan, 1946), 65.

Dying at a Fork in the Road: *Jim Elliot*
1. Elisabeth Elliot, *Through Gates of Splendor* (New York: Harper and Row, 1957), 59.
2. Robert Frost, "The Road Not Taken," 1920.

To a Girl in an Iron Lung: *A Hero Whose Name Is Withheld*
1. Elizabeth Longford, *Lord Byron* (Boston: Little, Brown, 1976), 44.

Score: God One, Cancer Zero: *Ormond Bentley*
1. William Shakespeare, *Hamlet*, Act 3, Scene 1.

The Very Stuff of Heaven: *Brittany Gilson*
1. These quotes are attributed to Anne Frank's diary, first published in The Netherlands in 1947 and since published in dozens of languages worldwide, including the first American edition, *Anne Frank: The Diary of a Young Girl*, in 1952.

A Wrinkle in Eternity: *Madeleine L'Engle*
1. Madeleine L'Engle, *Two-Part Invention* (New York: Farrar, Straus and Giroux, 1988), 231.
2. Ibid., 100.
3. Ibid., 229.
4. Ibid., 193.
5. Ibid., 195.

Entering Heaven from a Farmer's Pond: *To Dickey*
1. "Life's Railway to Heaven," 1890.
2. "Oh, Dem Golden Slippers," traditional African-American spiritual.

An Uncommon Man Beneath a Common Stone: *Bob Highfill*
1. Saint Justin, *Dialogue with Trypho the Jew*, in *The Early Christians in Their Own Words* (Farmington, Pa.: Plough Press, 1970), 298–99.

Scrubbing Up Saints: *Paul Little*
1. From the hymn "God Moves in a Mysterious Way" by William Cowper, 1731–1800.
2. Ibid.

The Look of Common Martyrs: *Martha Myers*

1. Personal correspondence from Martha Myers, September 1998.

Dinner in Anaheim: *Harold Shaw*

1. William Shakespeare, *King Lear*, Act 1, Scene 4.

2. Shakespeare, *The Two Gentlemen of Verona*, Act 1, Scene 2.

3. Luci Shaw, *God in the Dark* (Vancouver, BC: Regent College Press, 1978), 176–180.

4. Ibid.

Calvin Miller is a best-selling author with nearly four million books in print. Praised by such well-known voices as Max Lucado and Eugene Peterson, Miller speaks all over the world and is a former pastor and professor of preaching and pastoral ministry at Samford University's Beeson Divinity School. He and his wife make their home in Birmingham, Alabama.

WORTHY
P U B L I S H I N G

IF YOU LIKED THIS BOOK . . .

- Tell your friends by going to: www.letters-to-heaven.com and clicking "LIKE"

- Share the video book trailer by posting it on your Facebook page

- Head over to our Facebook page, click "LIKE" and post a comment regarding what you enjoyed about the book

- Tweet "I recommend reading #LettersToHeaven by Calvin Miller @Worthypub"

- Hashtag: #LettersToHeaven

- Subscribe to our newsletter by going to http://worthy publishing.com/about/subscribe.php

**WORTHY PUBLISHING
FACEBOOK PAGE**

**WORTHY PUBLISHING
WEBSITE**